An Introduction to
the American Underground Film

SHELDON RENAN was born in Portland, Oregon, in 1941. He became addicted to the film medium during his four years at Yale University, where he was a member of the Scholar of the House Program. After graduation in 1963, he spent much of his time scurrying from one movie theatre to another, and did not emerge from the darkness until 1966, when he married, wrote this book, and settled near San Francisco.

An Introduction to

THE AMERICAN
UNDERGROUND FILM

by Sheldon Renan

A Dutton  *Paperback*

New York
E. P. DUTTON & CO., INC.

Foreword

It is with very special pleasure that I respond to Sheldon Renan's invitation to write the foreword to his book. We met while we were screening films for THE INDEPENDENT FILM, the exhibition which introduced me as the new director of The Museum of Modern Art's Department of Film, and it was then that I first saw the avidity, energy, and dedication he brought to looking at films. This book is eloquent proof of his labors.

But why should a documentary film-maker comment on the underground film? We documentarists have been, and are, concerned with the presentation of the "real" world with special emphasis on its problems. From the beginning we have tried to involve the spectator in an experience that could lead to change. If there is a problem affecting a great many people, and there usually *are* problems affecting a great many people, why not make a film about it? Maybe someone will do something.

But the kind of film we might choose to make, the devices and techniques, the style of the photography, the approach to the sound track, have always been the subjects for exploration by the film-maker, whatever his persuasion. So we have that in common. And let us be clear, documentarists or any other kind of film-maker, we are all working on the problems of form and content, consciously or otherwise.

We begin and end with a dream. The beginning differs with each of us, but the final product is up there on the screen, in the form of moving shadows, for everyone to see. Just moving shadows. If you think they represent reality, that is your interpretation.

In the beginning, as Mr. Renan tells us, there were two film-makers who seemingly were very different. Lumière, convinced that photography was indeed the medium of realism, and Méliès, who assimilated it into his bag of magic tricks. They were blood brothers, as the final test proved, for audiences were moved by the shifting shadows created by both, and that was the idea the film-makers had in mind.

As a documentarist, I have always been slightly envious, however, of the artist who makes his personal statement without compromise. Films cost money, and to travel to underdeveloped places with camera and crew is beyond the resources of most film-makers. No matter how much one would wish to make an impassioned film plea for justice in the Congo, for instance, the direct experience of finding the appropriate images on the spot and transferring them to film is out of the question without substantial financial support from someone. And if such aid is forthcoming, it will be from sources that have a stake in the kind of film that is to be made. You have to be lucky to have a sponsor whose goal is the same as yours.

But if you have something to say, and only yourself to satisfy, the limitations are your skill, the persistence of your vision, and the availability of a little money. You may even destroy your work when you finish; it is yours, but if you share it with others, so much the better.

Mr. Renan has described many visual delights, but no matter how skillfully they may be used, words are no substitute for those elusive shifting shadows. This introduction to the underground film will help you to choose which ones suit your particular fancy.

WILLARD VAN DYKE

The Museum of Modern Art
New York, N.Y.

Preface

I was a compulsive movie-goer. Not a critic, really, and certainly not a scholar. I had exhausted the films available at the time in commercial theatres, and I went "underground" in search of more and different kinds of films to see. I wrote this book to aid me in my search.

I started looking in the Spring of 1965, and I started writing in the Spring of 1966. When I started writing, I stopped looking, and although some information was added, this is an introduction to the underground film as it was circa Spring 1966.

I did not manage to see all the films I have written about here. (Nor have I written about all the films I saw.) Especially with regard to the older avant-garde and experimental films, I relied heavily on the content of those sources mentioned in the bibliography.

Regarding the illustrations, most of the photographs in this book are pale (and frequently scratched) shadows of the films they represent. This is because they are frame blowups reproduced directly from the films. Illustrations of commercial films are never taken from the films themselves. They are posed photographs taken by a special "still" photographer on the movie set during the filming of the production. Underground film-makers, of course, cannot afford this expense. Hence the need for frame blowups.

The number of people imposed upon in the writing of this book was enormous. The cooperation given by the staffs of the Film-makers' Cooperative, the Film-makers' Cinematheque, Cinema 16, the Museum of Modern Art Department of Film, Audio Film Center, and the Creative Film Society was indispensable. Of the many individuals who gave information and aid I will mention only Jonas Mekas, Amos Vogel, Adrienne Mancia, Joseph Longo, Gretchen Berg, Jack Stauffacher, P. Adams Sitney, Ken Kelman, Eileen Bowser, Margareta Akermark, Standish Lawder, and, of course, the film-makers themselves. I never would have managed to start, let alone finish, the actual writing of this book without the constant encouragement of my wife Barbara. And both book and author would have been much thinner without the support of Arthur I. Cohen, the Renans, the Strosses, and for the final push, the Rockefeller Foundation.

SHELDON RENAN

El Cerrito, California

Contents

List of Illustrations

An Introduction to
the American Underground Film

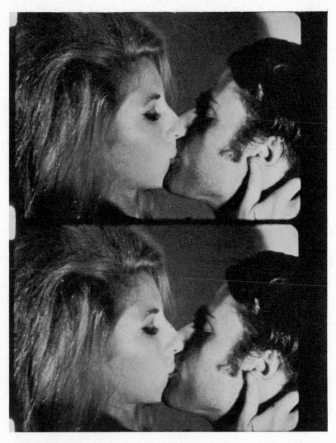

Andy Warhol's early films, like *Kiss*, have practically no movement.

ONE: What Is the Underground Film?

There are underground films in which there is no movement, and films in which there is nothing but movement. There are films about people and films about light. There are short, short underground films and long, long underground films. There are some that have been banned, and there is one that was nominated for an Academy Award. There are sexy films and sexless films, political films and poetical films, film epigrams and film epics.

Definitions are risky, for the underground film is nothing less than an *explosion* of cinematic styles, forms, and directions. If it can be called a genre, it is a genre that can be defined only by a cataloging of the individual works assigned to it. The film medium is rich with possibilities, and the underground film-maker has widely explored these possibilities, with the result that there are almost as many different kinds of underground films as there are underground film-makers.

The underground film *is* a certain kind of film. It is a film conceived and made essentially by one person and is a *personal statement* by that person. It is a film that dissents radically in form, or in technique, or in content, or perhaps in all three. It is usually made for very little money, frequently under a thousand dollars, and its exhibition is outside commercial film channels.

The term "underground film" belongs to the sixties, but the personal film is not a new phenomenon. It goes back almost to the beginning of film, a seventy-year tradition that has had many names, underground being only the latest. This contemporary manifestation, however, is of a greater magnitude than any before.

There are fantastic numbers of people now producing personal "art films," and at least a hundred of these are of known significance. Some are students. Some are artists known for work in other fields. Some are film-makers who do nothing except make films.

The reason for these numbers is not just the interest in film that has built up in America over the past years. It is also the fact that the materials of film have become easily available. The low cost of 8mm and 16mm allow anybody to make a movie. And the small cameras and fast films of the sixties allow a movie to be photographed almost anywhere.

The accessibility and portability of film has resulted in freedom. This means not just freedom to make films, but freedom to make them for purely personal satisfaction and to purely aesthetic standards. It means freedom to make complex films, intimate films, films close to life or made of dreams, films like poems and films like paintings. This is what the underground is all about.

To repeat, such films have been made before. But the making of them in such numbers, with such determination, and with so immediate a recognition is new. So is the degree of freedom. The underground film displays a variety, an intimacy, and a "lifefulness" that few commercial films have ever matched. The commercial film is a medium of and for bankers, craftsmen, film crews, and audiences. The underground film is a medium of and for the individual, as explorer and as artist.

Basic Film

The basis for all film, "above ground" or underground, is the film medium. Film is a *substance* on which, usually by photochemical processes, a sequence of images has been placed. Film is a *process* in which light is shown through the substance film, projecting on a surface the shadow of the image sequence printed on the film. Actually a series of still shadows, film produces the illusion of moving life.

The film process is simple, but it has yielded a medium

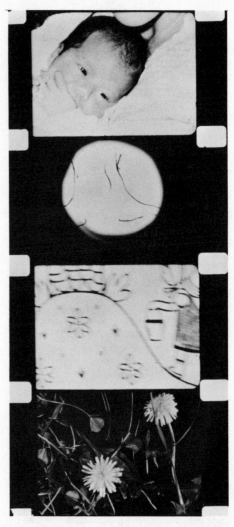

Almost every frame of Robert Breer's *Fist Fight* is discontinuous from every other, resulting in a sense of frantic movement.

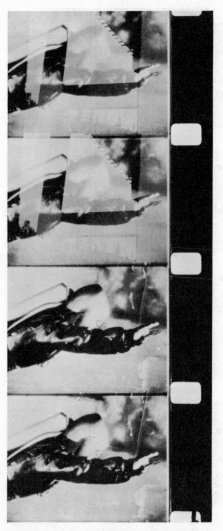

Bruce Baillie borrows Rocketman, a character from a grade-B
movie serial, to use as a symbol of a modern Don Quixote
flying across the American landscape (seen here in light
superimposition) in *Quixote*.

of tremendously rich effect. It offers the film-maker the use of form, of color, of movement, of plastic space, of time, and of sound. These qualities may be created and sensitively adjusted at different points in the making, including direction of action, photographing, developing, printing, and editing. Out of the qualities of form, color, and so on, the film-maker is able to produce a reality separate from real life. This new reality may be totally controlled, and it is quite persuasive. It looks real whether it resembles actual reality or not.

The film medium has the option of incorporating any other medium. Drama, literature, music, dance, painting, and photography may be part of a film, as well as dynamic variations therein. Film has a remarkable potential, and it has hardly been touched.

Out of the film medium come all the different kinds of film. One of these is the underground film.

Underground and Other Names

Again, one starts by saying, there is a certain kind of film. It is made by a single person. It is made primarily for reasons of personal or artistic expression. And it is always, by necessity, made with limited means. Avant-garde, experimental, independent, and underground are all terms used to describe this kind of film.

There have been three periods of exceptional achievement in this area of film-making. (With expanded cinema there begins a fourth.) These three periods are sometimes referred to as *the three film avant-gardes.*

The first film avant-garde was in the twenties. It rose out of modern art, especially dada and surrealism, and so the films, like the works of art, were called "avant-garde." Avant-garde, of course, means in the front rank, or the newest thing. Whenever a new kind of film appears it is called by this name. Thus this term is sometimes used to describe contemporary films. But its strongest reference is to those films of the twenties, works such as Clair's *Entr'acte*, Ray's *Emak Bakia*, and Buñuel/Dali's *Un Chien Andalou*, that were the predecessors of the underground film.

The second period was in the forties. Some works made then are now called underground. When they were produced, however, they were often called "experimental" films. Originally, in the twenties, *experimental* was a word used to describe the montage films of the Russians. But by the forties, it was the word for works such as Deren's *Meshes of the Afternoon*, Anger's *Fireworks*, and Peterson's *The Lead Shoes*. Experimental means part of a logical inquiry by trial and error. These films were called experimental for trying to do things that had not been done before. But the term was not accurate, because film-makers were artists expressing themselves and not scientists conducting a logical inquiry. Many film-makers objected also to the idea that their films were experiments and not finished works of art. The term, however, is still used to describe those films and films made today.

The third period began in the second half of the fifties and runs up to the present. Two terms have been popular in describing the personal film during this time, *independent* and *underground*.

Independent in this context means free of Hollywood. But the name has been taken by a variety of film-makers, including commercial film-makers who produce Hollywood-type films outside of the studio system. Many noncommercial independents have thus tended to dissociate themselves from the word.

Underground film was a term originally used by critic Manny Farber to describe low-budget masculine adventure films of the thirties and forties. But in 1959 the term began to have reference to personal art films. Lewis Jacobs, in an article called "Morning for the Experimental Film," in *Film Culture* (Number 19, Spring, 1959), used the words "film which for most of its life has led an underground existence." And film-maker Stan VanDerBeek says that he coined *underground* that year to describe his films and those like them. Whatever its source, the term came into general usage, for there was at the time a feeling that the forces that be were trying to keep this certain kind of film from being made. Underground described an attitude: the determination that the films should be made and should be seen despite all economic and legal barriers.

Many film-makers disavow the word *underground*, not liking its intimations of seediness and illegality. It *is* an inadequate term, and so are the rest. They are all attempts to group together various kinds of films that don't fit into other categories. The press, however, picked up the underground appellation because it made good copy. Exhibitors found more people would come to see "underground films" than would come to see something called "avant-garde" or "independent." *Underground film* has thus been absorbed into the national vocabulary.

There is one more term that is used interchangeably with "the underground film." This is "the New American Cinema." It is derived from the New American Cinema Group, an organization founded in 1960 by a number of independent film-makers whose work ranged from the commercial to the avant-garde. The New American Cinema takes in the underground film, but is broader than it. It is the total rebellion in the United States against the domination of film by Hollywood and other commercial factors.

Physical Dimensions

Underground films are of predictable width but unpredictable length.

An underground film is almost always 16mm or 8mm wide. The avant-garde films of the twenties were made in 35mm, but during the Second World War 16mm film came into extensive use. Sixteen-millimeter equipment was available and less costly than 35mm to use. It has been the staple of the personal art film ever since.

Underground films exist in 35mm. With the exception of some by Robert Breer, Stan VanDerBeek, and Harry Smith, however they were originally filmed in 16mm and blown up to 35mm. Alfred Leslie has filmed in 8mm and blown up to 35mm.

Eight-millimeter is even less expensive than 16mm, and its equipment is now the easiest of all to come by. Traditionally 8mm has been a home-movie medium, as well as one for beginners in creative film-making. Recently, however, accomplished film-makers have begun to explore (and explode) 8mm. Stan Brakhage with his *Songs*, Robert Branaman with his "rolls," Ken Jacobs, and others have broken down any supposed barriers that existed between home movies and works of art.

Commercial films are usually made a certain length in order to fit certain economic requirements. A feature, for

These strips of film show the actual size of (from l. to r.) 8mm, 16mm, and 35mm. 8mm is from a Stan Brakhage *Song*.

example, must be long enough for a patron to feel he is getting his money's worth, but no longer than he can comfortably sit through. Underground films are ruled by other economic requirements, namely production cost, so they are usually under thirty minutes in length. Aside from that, they are free to be whatever length their makers wish. Robert Breer's *A Miracle* is fourteen seconds long. Andy Warhol's portrait of the Empire State Building, *Empire*, is eight hours long.

Subject Matter

In classic French film criticism there are two basic kinds of film. There is the objective (documentary) film, theoretically originating from Louis Lumière. There is the subjective (fictive and transformatory) film, theoretically originating from Georges Méliès. It is generally assumed that film as art always falls under the second (fictive and transformatory) heading.

The work of the underground, however, is not limited to any given area of film-making, and in fact is sprawled across both categories. The underground film-maker tends to make films of things in his actual life (documentary), but he usually transforms their appearances and their importance (fictive and transformatory) in the process of filming and editing. He uses people and places from his own life, because they are what he has feelings about. But actual life for the underground film-maker may be only raw material to be manipulated into the form of his personal perspective.

Portraiture

Making portraits of family and friends is extremely popular in the underground. Most film-makers have done film portraiture, although with considerable variance in style. In Andy Warhol's *Henry Geldzahler*, for example, the subject lies on a couch nearly motionless while the camera grinds away for forty minutes. Brakhage, in one of his 8mm *Songs*, shows his daughter Crystal in many different moods, in different colors, in different environments. Ken Jacobs has made an 8mm film of Alfred Leslie and his family that is intercut with

This segment from Stan Brakhage's *15 Song Traits*, all portraits, shows his daughter Crystal.

bits from an ancient Mickey Mouse cartoon. The cartoon has to do with Mickey being separated from Minnie Mouse and then being reunited with her. Jacobs's portrait is in two parts. The first is called *Lisa and Joey in Connecticut* and shows Leslie while his wife and son are in Connecticut. The second is called *"You've Come Back!" "You're Still Here!"* and shows the Leslie family reassembled.

Brakhage especially has put much of his life, starting at age twenty, on film, and he has kept his film diary faithfully as he has raised his family. Most of his children were actually photographed as they were being born.

The underground film-maker makes portraits, too, of contemporary landscapes, attitudes, and events. Bruce Baillie's *Mass* and *Quixote* are quite consciously portraits of America, complicated film and sound montages that protest its uglinesses and memorialize its beauties. Jonas Mekas's *The Brig* and Kenneth Anger's *Scorpio Rising* both show an attitude of violence that saturates the sixties, and so does Bruce Conner's *Report*. *Report* is a montage of footage from the Kennedy assassination. It is a poetic document of that event, and of the effect it had on the nation and, of course, on Conner.

There is, as well, a tendency to document other works of art or to use them as a springboard. Mekas photographed *The Brig*, Kenneth Brown's play, as it was being performed by the Living Theater. Marie Menken's *Mood Mondrian* is Piet Mondrian's painting "Broadway Boogie Woogie" photographed and brought to life by Menken's moving camera. And there is practically a whole genre of films that are based on happenings, most notably Vernon Zimmerman's *Scarface and Aphrodite*, which is a photographed and shortened version of Claes Oldenburg's Happening called *Gayety*.

Protest

A significant minority of underground films includes protest (i.e., politics) in its subject matter. The favorite target is war, and nuclear war in particular, VanDerBeek's *Breath-death* and Ray Wisniewski's *Doomshow* being examples of such works. Other targets include segregation (Robert Nelson's *Oh Dem Watermelons*), military brutality (Mekas's *The Brig*), and the American status quo (Jacobs's *Star*

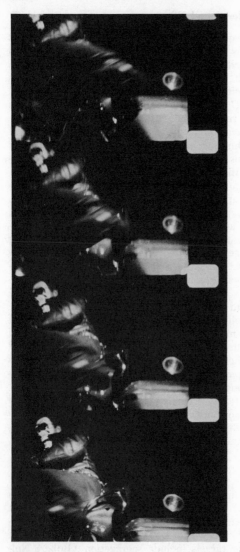

Death climbs on a motorcycle in Kenneth Anger's *Scorpio Rising*.

A burning jet fighter hurtles out of Secretary of Defense McNamara's face and down New York City's Park Avenue in *Quixote*.

A naked young lady dances frenetically midst splashes and bashes of light in Bruce Conner's *Cosmic Ray*.

Spangled to Death). The political orientation of underground film-makers seems to run from liberalism to all-out anarchy.

Sex

Much of the popularity of underground films is based on the expectation that they will include large dollops of sex. This expectation is sometimes rewarded. And sometimes it is not. There is more nudity in underground films than there is in commercial films. But there is less sex.

What sex there is tends to be less licentious, but the representation tends to be more uninhibited. In a commercial film, for example, the director will do a great deal of hinting. He will build to a suggestive incident, but will cut before anything happens. Or he will show a couple after they are supposed to have made love. He will dress women skimpily, but will cut out anything like a nipple or pubic hair. Or he will show the heroine in her bath from the shoulders up. In an underground film anybody taking a bath will probably be seen taking a bath. And couples may simply be having intercourse, naked in the center of the screen.

A homosexual director in Hollywood will make, however perverse, heterosexual films. An underground film-maker is more likely to follow his own inclinations. Other sexual relationships than strictly heterosexual ones may be shown. Whatever happens in real life or in the imagination of an individual can be shown in underground films. This is a freedom that personal film-makers have and that they occasionally exercise.

Cineplastics

There are films that, strictly speaking, do not have a subject. They are abstract or nonobjective. Their subject is their pattern, their rhythm, their sense of light and color.

Some are photographed, like Brakhage's *Pasht*. Some are painted directly on film, like Harry Smith's work from the early forties. Some are animated abstractions, like Robert Breer's form evolutions. Some, like Ed Emshwiller's *Dance Chromatic*, combine live action and animation.

The ultimate to date in the nonobjective film is Tony Conrad's *The Flicker*. It has only black and white frames.

They are alternated in varying patterns, and the resulting
strobe effect can set off strong reactions in the mind of the
viewer. It can cause the illusion of color, of a spreading of
light, and of lacy patterns. (To the unlucky one in 15,000
The Flicker will bring an attack of photogenic epilepsy.)

Magic

Starting with Georges Méliès, who was an illusionist by
trade, film has always had an attraction for those interested
in magic and the supernatural. The reality that is created on
film by the film-maker is very real. To look at it is to believe
it. On film one can do magical tricks and conjure apparitions
that, if by chance they should exist, stay invisible in real life.
Thus film, the most science-and-technology-based of the arts,
is the medium that gives most comfort to mystics and be-
lievers in magic.

Alchemy, magic, and the supernatural in general have a
surprisingly large role in the underground. Many film-makers
believe in the supernatural, several are practicing occultists,
and their belief is reflected in their work. Maya Deren, who
is sometimes called the Mother of the Underground Film,
was involved in the practice of Haitian voodoo, and started
a film, never finished, on the subject. Kenneth Anger, a
follower of the English occultist Aleister Crowley, intends
many of his films to be magical invocations. Storm de Hirsch's
Peyote Queen is very much like a ritual of incantation with
its drum-punctuated visual changes.

Makers of collage films seem to be especially involved
with magic. Harry Smith, who began learning about alchemy
from his father when he was fourteen, has an hour-long
collage film, called by Jonas Mekas *The Magic Feature*, that
is a series of transformations of supernatural natures. Quite
independently, Larry Jordan has produced similar works, and
VanDerBeek even considers his satirical collages magical.
VanDerBeek, in fact, likes to call himself "the godson of
Georges Méliès."

Seeing

The underground is greatly involved with the act of seeing.
Starting in the fifties with Robert Breer's work and that of

Brakhage, there has been a fascination with the question of how one sees, of what sight is. The concern is with both the physiological and philosophical aspects of seeing.

Curious to know what the eye would retain, Breer made his *Images by Images I*, a loop film with no continuity from frame to frame; that is, each frame is completely different from the one before and after it. (He found the eye discovers a pattern even where none exists.) Brakhage developed, over a series of films, the idea of "closed eye vision." He tried to put in his films a total vision, one encompassing physical, psychological, and poetic aspects of vision. To achieve this, Brakhage painted over his films, scratched them, cut rapidly back and forth to introduce memory, and used multiple exposures. A simple example of this idea is Robert Branaman's *Night Lights & Day Hi's*. Branaman filmed a landscape, then painted on the film patterns he may have seen in a psychedelic experience he had while filming. The viewer sees regular vision and psychedelic vision at the same time, a composite.

Conrad's flicker film can be considered as an experiment in seeing, too. In fact, Conrad was introduced to the possibilities of stroboscopic stimulation of the optic nerves in a Harvard physiology class. Gregory Markopoulos is experimenting with the possibility of stimulating certain odors with film, that is, affecting the nose through the eyes with light.

The Subject of Film

Another concern of the underground is the question: What is film? Warhol explores that question when he makes a film in which there is no movement. Breer explores it when he makes a film in which there is no continuity, i.e., he uses frame by frame cutting. Ken Jacobs explores it when he puts on a show that mimics with live shadows the appearance of a film. Andrew Noren explores it when a girl in *Say Nothing* walks up to the camera and sticks her finger against the lens. Here, her finger indicates, is where the reality of this film ends.

Nam June Paik makes *Zen For Film*, a clear film with no image whatsoever. Takehisa Kosugi runs the projector without film in it at all. "Expanded cinema" arrives with its integration into film of many techniques and processes never before considered to be film. This questioning of the medium never stops. And with every new kind of film, with every new technique, the underground enlarges the definition of what film can be.

Poetry

One might call many underground works "film poems," but that is an uneasy category. It is uneasy because there really is not a satisfactory definition of poetry, let alone film poetry. Let it be said, though, that these films frequently instill in the viewer a sense of poetry.

Certain works are directly related to the forms and rhythms of literary poetry. Charles Boultenhouse's *Handwritten*, for example, seems to be almost a visual transcription of a written poem. And Bruce Baillie's *Tung* shows a poem in subtitles as the film progresses.

Narratives

Narratives are rare in the underground, or at least only a few have received much attention. Stanton Kaye's *Georg* is about a disturbed individual who fights a losing battle with society's war establishment. Peter Goldman's *Echoes of Silence* shows a series of alienated people living lives oppressed by the city. The first is in the form of a film diary kept by the protagonist, the other a silent and compassionate detailing of several people's existences.

There is a large group of films that are parodies of Hollywood films. The best known of these are the works of the Kuchar brothers: their titles, *I Was a Teen Age Rumpot, A Town Called Tempest, The Lovers of Eternity,* and so on, give some idea of their approach. Rudy Burckhardt and Red Grooms have made Pop Art take-offs on Méliès's *Voyage dans la Lune* and James Whale's *Frankenstein.* They are titled *Shoot the Moon* and *Lurk.*

Beyond Categories

Many of the major works, like Brakhage's *Dog Star Man,* Jack Smith's *Flaming Creatures,* Jacobs's *Blonde Cobra,* and Rice's *Chumlum,* do not fit specific categorical molds. They have a calculated effect. They have things to say. They communicate attitudes and a sense of certain existences. They communicate a presence and almost a sense of personality. But every film is something unique. As Ken Jacobs once said, "Each work creates its own aesthetic."

Style

Most underground films have a look of informality. They appear, some of them, as if they could start anywhere or could stop at any point or might have kept on going after they ended. (VanDerBeek, after shooting large amounts of footage, actually does, as he puts it, "slice a film off like a sausage.") They have a sense of flow. And they exude the easy intimacy of a home movie.

In contrast to this informality is an intensity and a complexity that is unmatched by commercial films. An underground film-maker works over his films like a painter over a canvas. He fills it with images, colors, and sounds that have meaning for him. He rearranges and rearranges until the result has, for the film-maker himself, with all his knowledge of the footage involved, maximum impact and integrity. By the time the film is finished, it may be so full of images that anybody seeing it for the first time may be unable to recall what he has seen. (Stan Brakhage says that seeing one of his films once is like reading a Canto by Ezra Pound on the Times Square sign that flashes news bulletins.) Most underground works do, in fact, demand repeated viewings. And they may look better when seen on an editor, where the viewer can control the speed, than when viewed projected on a screen.

Editing is frequently abrupt. Rarely is a narrative line followed. It is what makes visual sense or poetic sense that the film-maker is after. The film-maker is interested in the reality of his feelings and of his perspective, not in the "official" reality of, say, *Gone With the Wind*.

The cutting rhythm tends toward the fast and the furious. The single-frame shot, that is, an image that is on the screen for only one twenty-fourth of a second, is not forbidden, and is frequently used by Markopoulos, Brakhage, and Breer. Both Breer and Brakhage have made whole films of nothing but single-frame shots.

Speed is compounded by the frequent use of multiple imposition and of separate editing going on at each level of imposition. In parts of *Dog Star Man* Brakhage uses four image sequences at once, one on top of another, in quadruple imposition.

Madness

It may be considered part of the style of the genre that many underground films are made with and communicate a sense of calculated madness. In *Senseless*, Ron Rice's collection of wild and powerful images, in Jack Smith's insane *Flaming Creatures*, in Ken Jacobs's nutty and nostalgic *Little Stabs at Happiness* is an urgent craziness and a surprising wit.

This is a time when man has moved towards the destruction of the individual by society and the destruction of society by nuclear holocaust. Such works are flagrant lashings out at this status quo. They are the voices, acts, and images of individual personalities completely destroying existing ideas of how and what people and things should appear on the screen.

Technique

It is usually assumed that the underground is a hotbed of technical innovation. And it is true that many new approaches to film are developed in this area. But it is also true that today there are few techniques exclusive to the underground. One may see in a television commercial as many avant-garde effects as one sees in a film shown at the Film-makers' Cinematheque in New York City. There are differences, but sometimes they are only differences in finish or in sense of integrity.

Stan Brakhage has, in his writings, given a good look at how a film-maker views his own technique as opposed to that used in conventional films. First Brakhage describes, in terms of art history, how he sees normal usage:

> We have the camera eye, its lenses grounded to achieve 19th-century Western compositional perspective (as best exemplified by the 19th-century architectural conglomera-

tion of details of the "classic" ruin) in bending the light and limiting the frame of the image just so, its standard camera and projector speed for recording movement geared to the feeling of the ideal slow Viennese waltz, and even its tripod head, being the neck it swings on, balled with bearings to permit that Les Sylphides motion (ideal to the contemplative romance) and virtually restricted to horizontal and vertical movements (pillars and horizon lines) a diagonal requiring a major adjustment, its lenses coated or provided with filters, its light meters balanced, and its color film manufactured to produce that picture post card effect (salon painting) exemplified by those oh so blue skies and peachy skins.*

Brakhage then tells some of the things he does to rock this nineteenth-century boat:

By deliberately spitting on the lenses or wrecking its focal intention, one can achieve the early stages of impressionism. One can make this prima donna heavy in performance of image movement by speeding up the motor, or one can break up movement in a way that approaches a more direct inspiration of contemporary human eye perceptibility of movement, by slowing the motion while recording the image. One may hand hold the camera and inherit worlds of space. One may over- or under-expose the film. One may use the filters of the world, fog, downpours, unbalanced lights, neons with neurotic color temperatures, glass which was never designed for a camera, or even glass which was, but which can be used against specifications, or one may go into the night with a specific daylight film or vice versa. One may become vice versa, the supreme trickster, with hatfuls of all the rabbits listed above breeding madly.†

Not all film-makers are so articulate as Brakhage. But they know that the usual static compositions, plodding pace, and slickness of surface they see in commercial films will· not

---

* As quoted by Jonas Mekas in "Notes on the New American Cinema," *Film Culture*, No. 24, Spring, 1962.
† *Ibid.*

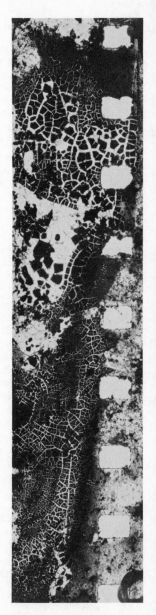

Mold grown on film by Brakhage is lacquered to preserve patterns and colors.

serve to communicate their feelings nor satisfy their aesthetic appetites.

Thus, when the film-maker films, he may do it with the camera held intimately in his hand, panning smoothly, rocking, or sailing in jittery dollies through space. Or he may, as Warhol did, place the camera firmly on a tripod and leave it there, unmoving, not moving, stock still for hours at a time. He may zoom back and forth in rhythm to a song. He may over- and under-expose on purpose. He may reexpose the same film again and again to make in-camera superimpositions. He may speed the film through the camera to get slow motion, or slow it to get fast motion.

Later he may paint the film. He may scratch into it. He may clip holes in it. He may, as Brakhage is now doing, grow mold on it to see what patterns appear.

When editing, the film-maker may put the splice in the middle of a frame so that it will jolt the eye when projected. He may edit the action so that it is more flashback than movement forward. He may, as Markopoulos does, show groups of single frame images, bursts of images like repeated phrases in a poem or a leitmotif in a musical composition. He may, as Robert Whitman did in a film prepared for his *Two Holes in the Water* Happenings, show simultaneously, in superimposition, both the front and the back of an action. Or he may, as both Brakhage and Branaman have done, make little film collages in individual frames, putting into a single frame actual pieces of film material from several different scenes.

The film-maker may make his film only of black frames and white frames, as Conrad did in *The Flicker*. He may put actual objects between mylar strips to make a film without photography, as Brakhage did with leaves and moth wings in *Mothlight*. He may splice together footage that he has not shot, footage made by different people for different reasons, footage compiled into a *film trouvé*, as Joseph Cornell did in the forties, and later Bruce Conner in his *A Movie*. He may take one image and project it over and over again, as in Landow's *This Film Will Be Interrupted After 11 Minutes by a Commercial*. Or he may, as the same film-maker did in *Fleming Faloon*, fill the frame with many little frames, each showing almost the same image.

He may project the film through a filter to alter its appear-

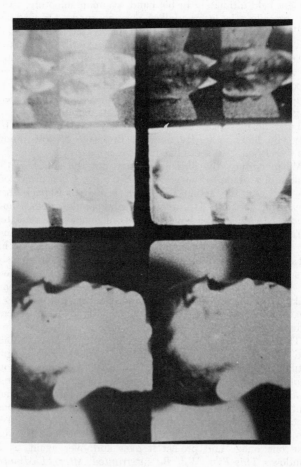

This *one* frame of George Landow's *Fleming Faloon* has ten little movies going on inside it.

ance. He may shape the image being projected with his hands. He may vary the speed of the projector, as Ken Jacobs does with certain footage, to make a film change in composition each time it is shown.

And so on.

Most of these techniques are not new. Griffith, it is said, had shots in *Intolerance* as short as five frames long. Méliès used many of these techniques, and so did Mack Sennett. When one sees slow motion, reverse motion, and mirror images in Clair's *Entr'acte*, they look fresh. But these techniques were, by the time of the first film avant-garde, already third hand. They look fresh in *Entr'acte* because they are serving a fresh sensibility.

So it is not the techniques that define the underground film, but the uses to which they are put. A television commercial uses a shaky camera to help sell some stereotype. An underground film uses it in a search for a freshness untouched by stereotypes. And intent strongly affects effect.

Roots of the Underground

The underground ferment resulted from many factors. Two important points have already been mentioned: the fact that a tradition of personal film-making had already been established by the avant-gardists of the twenties and the forties; and the fact that after the forties it became increasingly easy to gain access to the materials of film-making.

Certain of the avant-gardists, notably Hans Richter from the twenties and Maya Deren from the forties, acted as teachers, encouraging personal film-making as an alternative to working in the area of commercial cinema. Maya Deren provided the ideology for the coming generation with statements such as the following:

Cameras do not make films; film-makers make films. Improve your films not by adding more equipment and personnel but by using what you have to the fullest capacity. The most important part of your equipment is yourself: your mobile body, your imaginative mind, and your freedom to use both.*

* Maya Deren, "Amateur Versus Professional," *Film Culture*, No. 39, Winter, 1965.

Not all of the filmic influences leading to the forming of the underground were noncommercial. There were, for example, two European directors, Jean Cocteau and Roberto Rossellini, whose work was of considerable importance to Brakhage, Markopoulos, and other pioneers of the underground.

In the case of Cocteau, his *Orphée* and *La Belle et la Bête* were (and still are) films that were personal past all practicality and poetic with a vitality that surpassed preciousness. Cocteau reintroduced film as a medium that could transform objective reality into living, subjective poetry. With Rossellini, it was not only the films themselves, but the way they were made. *Open City* and *Paisan* were produced with catch-as-catch-can equipment, on the streets, sometimes as the very events they were about were actually happening. They were proof that out of imperfect conditions, out-dated film stocks, and little money *could come* powerful film art. Rossellini's films also reaffirmed how powerful the apparently objective camera could be. The films of Cocteau and Rossellini were distributed around the United States in the late forties and were seen by many who did not have access to the American experimental films.

Still another source of inspiration came from semicommercial directors in the United States who revolted against Hollywood in the fifties. These were people like Morris Engel, with his *Weddings and Babies*, and John Cassavetes, with *Shadows*. Essentially these films led to the "New York School" of low-budget features, but the spirit of revolt they generated was felt around the country.

The New Man

Just as the avant-garde films of the twenties came out of a climate of riotous anarchy, the underground films have issued from a volatile environment. In this case it is the climate of the new man.

In the fifties there developed in the United States a growing move toward personal freedom. Many began to dissent from the pressures of an increasingly oppressive societal environment. There was visible a willful withdrawal from cooperation with contemporary goals and modes of living. One example of this was the passive nonconformity of the

Jean Cocteau acted as a Méliès to young film-makers, introducing them to the promise of personal film fantasy with such films as *La Belle et la Bête*. (*Collection Museum of Modern Art Film Library*)

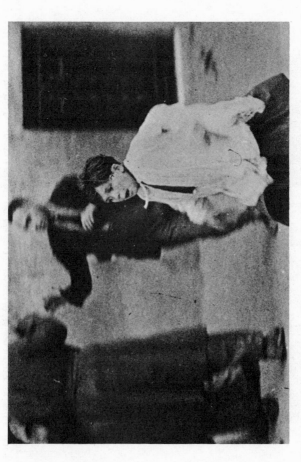

The power of Roberto Rossellini's neorealism in *Open City* affected both America's underground and France's *Nouvelle Vague*. (*Collection Museum of Modern Art Film Library*)

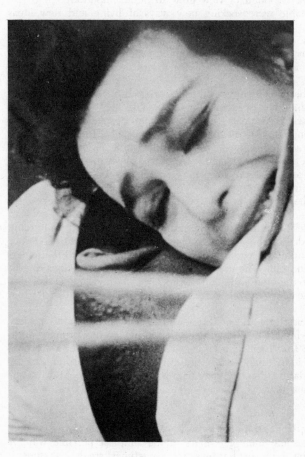

Shadows, filmed on actual locations as *Open City* was, created tremendous excitement among independent film-makers. (*Collection* Film Quarterly)

Beats, members of the so-called Beat Generation. Another was the increasing involvement with Eastern mysticism. The subjective point of view grew to be all important.

People were seeking new ways of living and new ideas about themselves. They attempted to liberate themselves from old perspectives. Hallucinogenic drugs came into frequent use. Out of this attempted expansion of definitions and consciousness, or at least along with it, came the idea of the "new man."

The new man is an explorer of ways of seeing and of existing. He is essentially responsible not to society but to himself. His goal is the fulfillment of his own individual vision, not the playing of a societal role. Ideally, the new man sees more, feels more, is willing to experience more than the "conventional man." He is the new species for a new age, and he is prepared for a future that will witness unprecedented changes.

The new man and the underground film developed together. The climate of the new man, in which to be new is to be desirable, in which the individual is constantly re-forming his idea of the world, in which the personal point of view is all important, was one of the factors that produced the underground film. The underground film, with its conscious dissent from the standards and approaches of the commercial film, is the film equivalent of the new man and his dissent from society.

It is the world of the new man, almost a separate society of sympathetic individuals, that provides the primary audience for these films. For, with his commitment to freedom and individuality in a time of increasing imprisonment by standardization, the new man has necessarily been an underground man.

How Underground Films Are Made

Personal films get made in the simplest possible way. A person buys or borrows (or sometimes steals) a camera, usually something on the order of a 16mm Bolex. He buys or borrows, et cetera, film. He begins to shoot.

He knows the resulting film will not make great amounts of money, so in lieu of professional actors, he uses family or friends. Unable to afford sets, he uses the real world. Narratives are usually improvised. In the case of non-narrative works, the film-maker simply "takes" images of the things around him.

He shoots when he can afford to, and when he feels like it, and when he can get the necessary materials and people together. Mekas's *The Brig*—which used an already existent stage play, set, and rehearsed actors—was shot, edited, and screened in three successive days. More usual, however, is the film that takes months or years to make. Goldman's *Echoes of Silence* was two years in the making; Brakhage's *Dog Star Man* five years.

The photographing is often done by the film-maker, and the editing always. He works with the most basic and inexpensive tools. And sometimes he cannot afford those. Markopoulos edited *Psyche* with magnifying glass, scotch tape, and a razor blade. Ken Jacobs used the same for his first film. It is only recently that equipment pools have been started on both coasts.

Processing and optical printing is usually handled by commercial film laboratories. More experienced film-makers, such as Brakhage and Emshwiller, may supervise or actually do much of their own lab work.

Sound, if used, is added later. Only a few films, such as *The Brig* and some of Warhol's work, have been shot with synchronized sound.

Animated films are done with improvised animation stands. (An animation stand is a construction that holds a camera firmly over a "table" on which the drawings or objects to be animated are placed for photographing. Some stands are quite large, as high as twelve feet.) Robert Breer's first stand, for instance, was made with a lobster crate (resulting in a stifling odor whenever the photo floodlights were on). Later he had a stand attached to his bed. When the mattress came off, the filming went on, and vice versa.

Some underground films enjoy more luxurious productions. Stanton Kaye's *Georg* was made with a nonprofessional crew. And it had full-scale mock-ups of Nike missiles, built by the leading lady, whose bread-and-butter job was with the National Space Administration. Andy Warhol uses a crew for all his films, the same people who produce his art for him. His studio in New York City is a sort of junior sound stage.

But having a crew to assist does not insure a better film.

Many of the best film-makers, Bruce Baillie, Stan Brakhage, Bruce Conner, et al., work alone.

Many film-makers would make films Hollywood-style if they could. Many would certainly prefer to work in 35mm or 70mm, to have dollies and cranes to photograph with, to have professional actors, to be able to screen rushes before shooting the next day, to afford retakes and fancy optical effects. But the film-maker who declares freedom from outside control, unless he has unlimited wealth, has to accept economic limitations. To some extent, underground film-makers make films the way they do because this is what they can do with the money they have available.

It is dogma in the underground, and partly true, that the disadvantages of the underground have their advantages. If the film-maker does not have klieg lights, 35mm cameras, dollies, and other tools of the commercial film profession, he does have small 8mm and 16mm cameras, fast film that does not need klieg lights, and a body to use as dolly and boom. If the film-maker cannot afford a crew of film technicians, he can do everything himself. Thus he is able to control every step of production. He is able to shoot quickly and quietly. And he becomes more intimately involved with the actual process of filming, and more sympathetic to the camera's eye.

For good or for bad, the underground film-maker is a man alone. But he is a man free to decide. This is a prerequisite to the making of art.

Craftsmanship

It is one of the myths about underground films that they are categorically poorly made. This *is* a myth, one believed by people who have not seen the span of underground work.

It is possible to see why the myth exists. Often films are highly praised and widely shown that *are* full of technical faults. And technically competent films may use unconventional techniques in which it is difficult to judge craftsmanship by conventional standards. Then, too, some film-makers purposely seek an amateurish look for their films.

A personal film-maker often starts without prior filming experience. His first works are always technically rough, but in some cases they may be important enough to warrant attention. Ron Rice's *The Flower Thief* is mostly overexposed and informally edited, but it has images of considerable power and a gentle poetry that is unique. Peter Goldman's *Echoes of Silence* is often underexposed, but it succeeds nevertheless in presenting the oppressive weight of life in a big city. Both of these films have a value above mere craftsmanship. Both will find a place in film history despite their technical faults. (And the particular technical faults in these films, the lightness in *The Flower Thief* and the darkness in *Echoes of Silence*, add to the effectiveness of the works.)

The struggle of the personal film-maker for technical quality is a difficult one. He is often using inferior materials. (One reason *The Flower Thief* is constantly overexposed is that it was filmed with the cheapest available raw stock: war surplus fighter-plane machine-gun film.) But the film-maker learns with experience how to achieve quality within the economic limitations the genre inevitably demands.

Many people in the underground can, in fact, get whatever they wish out of a camera. Stan Brakhage, Marie Menken, and Ed Emshwiller are all top technicians. By way of proof, it may be pointed out that all these people have done "professional" work: Emshwiller makes films for the United States Information Agency. Menken, who actually hand-holds the camera for her complex time-lapse films, was once a special effects expert for the Signal Corps. Brakhage worked in many different aspects of the film industry. If the camera jiggles in a Brakhage film, it is not a mistake; it is because he wanted it to jiggle, and in that precise way. If certain scenes in Baillie's *Mass* are overexposed, it is because he wanted them so exposed, and to that degree.

Then there are the films that look amateurish on purpose. Ken Jacobs made *Little Cobra Dance* and *Afternoon Blood Sacrifice* so that they gain a certain sense of scabrous vitality from their lack of technical finish. Jack Smith did the same with *Flaming Creatures*. Stanton Kaye's *Georg* incorporates its technical faults into its structure by being presented as a home movie by a man who compulsively records his life on film.

There is little of the supposed distaste for craftsmanship in the underground. What does exist is a distaste for films that exhibit craftsmanship to the exclusion of meaning, of art, of any sense of life. The film-maker seeks control and a sense of finish as much as any Hollywood cinematographer or

Peter Emanuel Goldman's *Echoes of Silence* won a prize at a European film festival and much praise, despite its technical faults.

director. If the underground result does not resemble the commercial result, it may be because a different result was desired, and not because the underground work is an inferior one.

The Importance of the Underground Film

Some underground films are good. Some are bad. A few are great. But whatever they are, underground films are the film artist's unmitigated vision. No banker, no producer, no patron has dictated what they must be or can later change them. Underground films are banned, but they are never cut.

Therefore the underground is free to look outward with an unblinking eye and inward in complex and mystical ways. It is free to be poetic and to be obscure. It is even free to go mad.

The underground film has a vitality, an arrogant originality, and an integrity that today is almost unique in cinema. It has unleashed the artist in the young and still unexplored medium of film. And the result has been *Dog Star Man, Quixote, Scorpio Rising, The Magic Feature, Relativity,* and hundreds of other films that could not have existed except in this separate world of film-making.

The underground has many forms, and some are being absorbed into the commercial cinema. Commercial cinema has always used the personal art film as a laboratory culture to be watched for usable material. As it adopted surrealism from *Un Chien Andalou,* as Walt Disney hired Oskar Fischinger to work on *Fantasia,* as Saul Bass used John Whitney to produce the titles for *Vertigo,* so will the underground find its techniques and ideas taken over. But this is of secondary importance.

The real importance of the underground is in its works. Alive, unpredictable, complex, and above all, personal, they are what is happening in cinema *now.* Their many forms are the true shapes of the vision of the contemporary individual.

Georges Méliès blows up his own head in his 1902 trick film *L'Homme à la Tête en Caoutchouc* (*The Man with the Rubber Head*). (*Collection Museum of Modern Art Film Library*)

TWO: A History of the
Avant-Garde/Experimental/Underground
Film in America

The history of the avant-garde/experimental/underground film in America does not begin in America. It begins in France, in the work of a professional magician, Georges Méliès.

The motion picture was invented to reproduce movement, to reproduce reality, to reflect like a mirror what went on before the lens of the camera. Film was primarily objective until Méliès stumbled upon the transformatory possibilities of the medium.

This happened as he was filming a view of traffic in Paris. His camera jammed for a minute, and after he developed the film, Méliès discovered that the bus that was on the scene when the camera stopped was magically transformed into a hearse that was in the bus's place when the camera started again. Following this invention, by accident, of stop-motion photography, he went on to discover fading, dissolving, masking, superimposition, slow motion, fast motion, and reverse motion. In short, he learned how to use film to manipulate reality.

Méliès's films were commercial successes. They were also works of totally personal art. He wrote the scripts, designed and painted the sets, ran the camera, directed the action, and sometimes even played the lead role. From 1896 to 1913, he made hundreds of films, most of them stagey spectacles such as *Voyage dans la Lune* (1902). Action in Méliès's films was restricted to sets of proscenium stage dimensions, however, and he was driven out of business when others made more dynamic and realistic use of the camera. Many contemporary underground film-makers have adopted Méliès as a progenitor and hero.

A number of other trick film-makers imitated Méliès and expanded his techniques. Among those who led to the founding of the avant-garde in France were Émile Cohl and Jean Durand. Cohl used trick techniques to animate objects, as in his hilarious *La Course aux Potirons* (1907), where pumpkins run wild in the streets. He also made some of the first films with animated drawings, for example, *Joyeaux microbes* (1909). Durand was a maker of comedies such as *Onésime Horloger* (1912), which used fast motion to tell the story of a man who speeds up time to gain an inheritance in a hurry.

Both Durand and Cohl had worked as assistants to Louis Feuillade, called the French Griffith. The dadaists were enthralled with Feuillade's mysterious detective serials, including *Fantômas* (1913), *Les Vampires* (1915), and *Judex* (1917). André Breton and Louis Aragon wrote, "In *Les Vampires* will be found the great reality of the century."

In America it was the time of "The Golden Age of Comedy." Though less artistic than the films of innovators such as Edwin S. Porter, D. W. Griffith, and Thomas Ince, the slapstick works of Mack Sennett were greatly admired by the avant-garde. Sennett and the other makers of silent comedies used to photograph their films on the streets of Hollywood. They would improvise with whatever was happening at the time, and later would edit with a great sense of timing. Their films were full of surprising poetry, visual tactileness, and a sense of immediacy that more serious films lacked. They presented, as Arthur Knight has said, "a world of ordered insanity."

The Avant-Garde Film

After the First World War, the world was filled with unrest—economic, social, political, and cultural. With traditional points of view fractured by post-War traumas, the ground was fertile for new ideas. On one hand, there was

Feuillade's mystery serial *Les Vampires* inspired the Surrealists. (*Lincoln Center Film Department*)

This production still of the cast of *Murphy's I.O.U.*, from Mack Sennett's Keystone Studios, exudes the wackiness that delighted dadaists. (*Collection Museum of Modern Art Film Library*)

discontent with the failings of commercial films, most evident in the writings of Louis Delluc, in France, who founded serious film criticism in 1919. On the other hand, modern artists were becoming interested in the film medium.

Out of these factors came a new kind of film. This development was summed up by Hans Richter in his history of the movement, which appeared in the *Art in Cinema* catalog, published by the San Francisco Museum of Art in 1947.

> In the ten years between 1921 and 1931 there developed an independent artistic movement in cinematography. This movement was called *Avantgarde*. . . . This art movement in film was parallel to such movements in plastic arts as Expressionism, Futurism, Cubism, and Dadaism. It was noncommercial, nonrepresentational, but international.

Germany

The climate in Germany was especially good, for the film industry there was, at the start of the twenties, producing the highly creative expressionist features. These were works such as Robert Wiene's *The Cabinet of Doctor Caligari* (1920), where the fantastic sets express the insanity of the point of view, Fritz Lang's super-symbolic *Destiny* (1921), and F. W. Murnau's version of the Dracula story, *Nosferatu* (1922). These were officially not avant-garde productions, and they tended to be heavy handed and self-consciously "arty." But they were of immense influence.

It was in Germany that the first films were made that today would be called "underground." They were the work of three painters, Viking Eggeling, originally from Sweden, Hans Richter, and Walter Ruttmann.

Eggeling and Richter were living together and were working along approximately the same lines. They worked for three years on scroll paintings that involved series of figures in sequences, somewhat like frames of an animated film. In 1920 UFA, a major German film production company, let them try to animate one of Richter's thirty-foot-long scrolls, but this proved unsuccessful.

Richter switched to animating on film a set of paper squares of all sizes and shades. The developed print of this experiment was covered with finger prints. But the negative

Nobody accused the actors of underacting in *The Cabinet of Doctor Caligari*, the best known of German Expressionist films that preceded the avant-garde. (*Collection Museum of Modern Art Film Library*)

looked clean when projected, and the negative became *Rhythmus 21* (1921). He went on with *Rhythmus 23* (1923) and *25* (1925), and *Film Study* (1926), which used "abstract forms related to and transformed into objects." He made many advertising shorts and documentaries, and continued his personal film-making with *Ghosts Before Breakfast* (1927–28), a delightful dada comedy that starred composers Paul Hindemith and Darius Milhaud. Later, having fled to the United States from the Nazis, Richter made *Dreams That Money Can Buy* (1944–46) and *8 x 8* (1957), two feature-length surrealist variety shows that exude a curiously archaic atmosphere.

Eggeling stuck to the difficult work of animating scroll paintings, assisted by a girl friend who learned the technique especially for him, and produced *Diagonal Symphony* (1921). He is said, however, to have made only two more films, *Parallèle* (1924) and *Horizontale* (1924), before his death in 1925.

Walter Ruttmann, working independently of Eggeling and Richter, produced a series of *Opus* films (1921–25) that had animated manipulations of geometric forms. Some of the films were colored by hand. Ruttmann did an animated dream sequence for Fritz Lang's *Die Nibelungen* (1924), but was most influential with his experimental documentary *Berlin, the Symphony of a Great City* (1927). Actually a successful commercial production, it showed a day in the city of Berlin, organized with attention to plastic continuity and rhythm. It caused the public to value the avant-garde lessons of treating material with an abstract eye. It also resulted in a slough of other "city symphonies." Ruttmann himself continued with *Weekend* (1928), which was a sound montage with no pictures, and *Melody of the World* (1929), another impressionistic documentary that led, for him, to increasingly commercial documentaries.

In *Melody of the World* were sequences of abstract forms animated as illustrations of classical and modern music. These were worked on by Oskar Fischinger, a painter who started animating films abstractly as the result of diagramming the emotional movements of a play by Shakespeare. Fischinger had produced animated advertising films starting in 1925, and then did a series of "absolute" films, calling them *Study No. 1, Study No. 2,* and so forth, animating to sound track

Hans Richter used superimpositional glass eyeballs in *Film Study*. (*Collection Standish D. Lawder*)

music from *Study No. 6* (1929) on, up to *Study No. 12* (1930). After *Colorature* (1931), he began to work in color, producing *Composition in Blue* (1933) and *Circle* (1933) before leaving Germany for the United States.

Another film considered part of the German avant-garde was *Uberfall* (1929) by Erno Metzner. This is a realistic tale of robbery and murder. When the main character is struck on the head, distorting mirror images are used to show his falling away from reality.

France

As can be seen, the avant-garde included more than simply personal art films. It was intimately involved with the commercial documentary and even the commercial story film. Jacques Brunius has classified the avant-garde in France into three phases. The first two were primarily commercial, the equivalent of today's official art films from Hollywood and Europe, and contributed little to the personal art film. The third, "The School of Paris," continues as an influence even today.

The first phase was contained in a single individual, Louis Delluc. Besides being a critic and a writer of scripts for Dulac and Cavalcanti, Delluc directed three dramatic films, *Fièvre* (1922), *La Femme de nulle Part* (1922), and *L'Inondation* (1924). It was Delluc, admittedly more with his critical writings than with his films, who lit the avant-garde fuse in France before he died in 1924.

The second phase contained narrative films of literary origin that utilized a certain amount of "trick" techniques—superimposition, soft focus, and striking camera angles. Germaine Dulac is included in this phase with her sullen psychological portrait of a house wife, *La Souriante Madame Beudet* (1922). Marcel L'Herbier is included with his *Feu Mathias Pascal* (1924) and *L'Inhumaine* (1925). Jean Epstein is considered a part of the second phase with many works, among them the overly romantic *La Chute de la Maison Usher* (1928) based on several stories by Edgar Allan Poe.

Another three directors were also included, Claude Autant-Lara, Jean Renoir, and Abel Gance. Autant-Lara made an experimental narrative, *Fait-Divers* (1924), and did a version of Jack London's *How To Start a Fire* (1928–

29) that used three frames placed side by side on film 45mm wide. Jean Renoir's films of the avant-garde period included *Charleston* (1926) and the costume fairy tale *Petite Marchande d'Allumettes* (1927).

Abel Gance has been attached to the second phase presumably because nobody knows quite what to do with him otherwise. Long before the start of the avant-garde he made an experimental science-fiction film, *La Folie du Docteur Tube* (1916), involving extensive distortion photography. In *J'Accuse* (1919) he had dead soldiers rise up in superimposition over their bodies on the battle field. And in the epic *Napoléon* (1925–27), he used three separate screens, the beginning of his "Polyvision" process. Gance is a giant, but one does not know whether he is a good giant or just a giant, for his films are rarely shown in America.

Also somewhat unique was Dimitri Kirsanov with his *Ménilmontant* (1924). Working almost entirely alone, and really part of neither the second nor the third of Brunius's phases, Kirsanov filmed a melodramatic story of a girl orphaned, seduced, and avenged, and did it with a hand-held camera in which he created striking montages and lyric superimpositions. It was poetic, it was touching, and it was original. *Ménilmontant* starred a beautiful Russian unknown, Nadia Sibirskaia, who later appeared in his *Brumes d'Automne* (1926), a film poem with rain, mist, autumn landscapes, and Sibirskaia's face with tears. Kirsanov made only one other independent film, a sound feature called *Rapt* (1933), which experimented with visual and audio counterpoint. He directed, before his death in 1957, a number of semicommercial and commercial films, of which he favored three shorts, the moody *Arrière Saison* (1952), the satiric yet ominous hunt film *Mort D'un Cerf* (1954), and *Deux Amis*, based on a story by Maupassant.

The School of Paris

The third phase of the French avant-garde had film-makers who alternated commercial and avant-garde productions and others who made strictly noncommercial works. The first group included René Clair, Alberto Cavalcanti, and Luis Buñuel, who became well-known directors. The second group included painters such as Fernand Léger, Man Ray, and

A ballerina tromped down on the camera, then turned up with a beard, in René Clair's *Entr'acte*. (*Collection Standish D. Lawder*)

Marcel Duchamp, who were interested only in extending into film their ideas as artists.

René Clair's first film was a commercial comedy called *Paris qui Dort* (1923) about a mad scientist who has frozen time for all the people in Paris except a group of adventurers living at the top of the Eiffel Tower. This wacky piece, with its references to early French trick films, was directly followed by the even wackier *Entr'acte* (1924), with a script by dadaist Francis Picabia and inspiration by Mack Sennett. It was made for the intermission of a Swedish ballet titled *Relâche*, which means "no performance today." *Entr'acte* is free from logic, being mostly about a chase after a runaway hearse, and the only reference to ballet are shots, straight up, of a bouncing ballerina who turns out to be bearded. Among the actors were Man Ray, Marcel Duchamp, and the composer Erik Satie. Following this triumph, Clair went back to making commercial films, great ones.

Man Ray, a painter who supported himself with photography, made in one day a short film called *Le Retour à la Raison* (1923). This return to reason was entirely reasonless, containing film ray-o-grams, that is, pictures made by objects set directly on film that was then exposed to imprint their outlines. It also included shots of a field of daisies and other common things in an uncommon context. The film, shown the evening after its creation at a dadaist program, caused so violent a reaction in the audience that it had to be stopped before its three minutes were through. Ray made a similar but more ambitious work called *Emak Bakia* (1926), the title meaning, in Basque, "leave me alone." It included many abstract and not so abstract forms moving in light and had a remarkable sequence where the famous model Kiki, staring at the camera, opens her eyes to reveal that the first pair of eyes are simply painted on her lids. His *L'Étoile de Mer* is an abstruse love story photographed through distorting glass with titles from a poem by Robert Desnos. *Les Mystères du Château du Dé* (1929) is a surrealist mystery film, a picturesque game improvised by Ray while a guest at the château of the Comte de Noailles (who later paid for the production of both *Le Sang d'un Poète* and *L'Age d'Or*).

In most of the avant-garde films, from Man Ray's early films to the commercial documentaries, such as Ruttmann's *Berlin*, the objective pictorial material becomes submissive

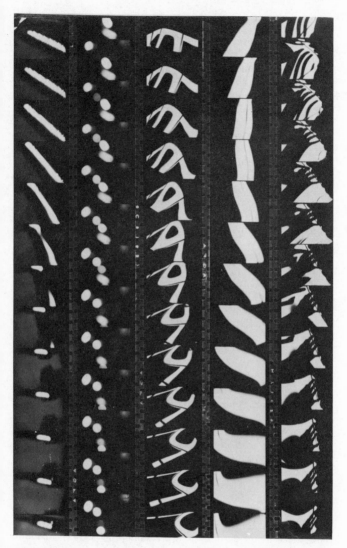

Man Ray used rotating objects to reflect patterns of light in
Emak Bakia. (*Collection Standish D. Lawder*)

to its plastic and rhythmic character. Louis Delluc had written in 1920, "Not enough attention is paid to photogenic objects. A telephone, for instance. . . ." And also, "I have seen an admirable technical phenomenon. I have seen cadence." And again, "Light above everything else is the question at issue . . . a director must realize that light has meaning." This consideration of the abstract factors, to the point of making them the content of films, was what raised the experiments of the School of Paris to importance.

The great cubist painter Fernand Léger, with the technical help of an American named Dudley Murphy, made *Le Ballet Mécanique* (1924), a montage of objects and movements. In it pots, pans, the repeated images of a fat woman climbing stairs, and so on, are edited into a visual dance of mechanical rhythms. Eugene Deslaw followed this with his *Marche des Machines* (1928), a pattern film featuring machinery, and his *La Nuit Electrique* (1930) with night lights.

Some of the avant-garde works were no more than documentaries with rhythmic cutting principles applied. Jean Epstein experimented, for study purposes at private ciné clubs, with rhythmic editing of essentially documentary footage in *Photogénie* (1925). But the most influential such work was Alberto Cavalcanti's *Rien que des Heures* (1926), an impressionistic view of twenty-four hours of life in Paris. More dramatic but less symphonic in form than the German *Berlin*, which it slightly preceded, *Rien que des Heures* was followed by *En Rade* (1928), Cavalcanti's sentimental documentary of a harbor.

Joris Ivens, in Holland, made similar, though slightly purer films, *The Bridge* (1928), *Rain* (1928), and *Branding* (1929), a film poem about waves. Georges Lacombe, Clair's cinematographer, made a documentary about a Paris market, *La Zone* (1929). And Jean Vigo's social critique *À propos de Nice* (1927–29), made with Boris Kaufman, was considered an avant-garde documentary at that time.

Because of their great emphasis on plastic and rhythmic values, the avant-garde films were sometimes called "absolute cinema," and sometimes "pure cinema." René Clair's brother, Henry Chomette, actually made a film called *Cinq Minutes de Cinéma Pur* (1926), and also *Reflets de Lumière et de*

Vitesse (1925), both of which were nothing more than footage reflected through moving crystals, edited for rhythm.

Some of the films lacked apparent meaning. Marcel Duchamp's *Anaemic Cinéma* (1927) was composed entirely of spirals with sentences of poetic homonyms inscribed around them. This film was actually part of a series of experiments by Duchamp in an attempt to produce stereoscopic films.

Others were heavily laden with meaning, as the Freudian and surrealistic *La Coquille et le Clergyman* (1928). This was directed by Germaine Dulac from a scenario by Antoine Artaud, and the scenario was said to be better than the film. The film was effective enough, however, to be turned down by the British Board of Censors with the comment: "The film is so cryptic as to be almost meaningless. If there be a meaning, it is doubtless objectionable." (Dulac strangely reversed the usual process of proceeding from experimental to commercial films. Her early films were commercial features, and her last films, before she went to the making of newsreels, were abstract poems of forms set to music, *Disque 957* and *Rhythme et Variations* [1930].)

The most famous avant-garde film of all was actually a violent reaction against the overly apparent artistic formalism of avant-garde films. This was the surrealistic *Un Chien Andalou* (1928), directed by Luis Buñuel after a scenario by Buñuel and Salvador Dali. Eyes that had been soothed with rhythmic compilations and amused by tricky superimpositions in other avant-garde films were now assaulted with vicious block-buster images. In the film an eye is sliced with a razor. Putrifying donkeys are dragged through a room. A man is suddenly clutching at the bare buttocks of a woman. The images are strung together in an almost nonexistent story. "NOTHING, in this film," Buñuel later assured, "SYMBOLIZES ANYTHING." The avant-garde that the film was meant to affront hailed it as a masterpiece.

Buñuel then made, again with limited collaboration with Dali, the feature-length *L'Age d'Or* (1930). This violently realistic and surrealistic story of sex and inhibition was in sound and had a score by Buñuel himself. Its showing caused a riot complete with bombs. It was banned and then most of its prints destroyed. It is said to be a masterpiece, but its influence has naturally been curtailed by its limited exposure.

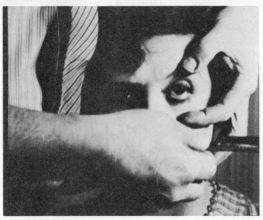

The most famous scene in avant-garde films is in *Un Chien Andalou*, where Luis Buñuel smokes a cigaret, holds open a girl's eye, and after a cloud has crossed the moon, slices open the eye. (*Collection Standish D. Lawder*)

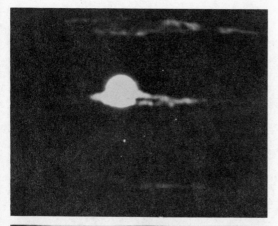

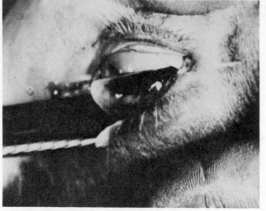

The heroine of Luis Buñuel's *L'Age d'Or* kisses a statue's toe.
(*Collection Standish D. Lawder*)

At the same time as *L'Age d'Or* was being finished, Jean Cocteau, a Jack-of-all-Arts, was making another surrealist sound feature, *Le Sang d'un Poète* (1930). This is a tremendously complex work, an allegory about the life of a poet (Cocteau had once called it *La Vie d'un Poète*) that uses all the trickster techniques of cinematic transformations the avant-garde had rediscovered. Statues come alive. Living beings become statues. Some personages are part people, part sculpture, and part drawing. The production was remarkably photographed by a great cinematographer, Georges Perinal.

As has been mentioned, the avant-garde was international. There was Len Lye from New Zealand, making the animated *Tusalava* (1928) while living on a houseboat in London. There was Kenneth MacPherson, also in England, who made a psychoanalytic narrative called *Foothills* (1929), *Monkeys' Moon* (1930) about escaping monkeys, and *Borderline* (1931), another psychoanalytic film, starring Paul Robeson. Joris Ivens was working in Holland. And a Belgian painter named Francis Brugière made *Light Rhythms* (1930), a sound short that used moving lights to give the appearance of movement to abstract paper sculptures.

Russia

Russia produced a strange version of the avant-garde spirit. When the Revolution of 1917 succeeded, the small film industry that had existed there was gone. Lenin, declaring that "Of all the arts, cinema is the most important for us," started a new one, and the state provided considerable money for experiment in film. The two Russians who had the most effect on the European and American avant-garde were Dziga Vertov and Sergei Eisenstein.

Dziga Vertov (born Dennis Kaufman, brother of the cinematographer Boris,) established the point of view that the eye of the camera, the "kino-eye," saw a reality that was different and superior to the reality seen by the human eye. He taught that the reality of the kino-eye, with its freedom to control time, space, and content, should not be restricted to representation of human eye reality. Thus he introduced the trick techniques to the Soviet Union. He did not see them as fictionalizing but as creating a new reality.

Vertov, in fact, was against the fiction film and sought to make only films of actuality. He was the main director of Russian propaganda documentaries. He produced *History of the Civil War* (1921), the magazines in the form of film called *Kino-Pravda* (1923–25), *Kino-Eye* (1924), *Forward Soviet* (1926), *The Sixth Part of the World* (1926), which intertwined scenes from the Western and Soviet countries, the famous *Man with a Camera* (1929), and among others, two sound features, *Enthusiasm* (1930) and *Three Songs about Lenin* (1934). Vertov predicted the techniques of *cinéma vérité* and helped innovate many of them. His influence on world cinema was great, and many of the film ideas of the contemporary underground cinema parallel his of forty years ago.

Sergei Eisenstein left the Russian theatre to make films, his first being *Strike* (1924), an expressionist film with jerky power and a bag of tricks. Then, in two months' time, he made *Potemkin* (1925), the film that introduced "the Russian style of editing" to the Western world. *Potemkin's* effect was immediate, and shows, for example, in the opening passages of Ruttmann's *Berlin*. Eisenstein next made *October* (1927), also called *Ten Days That Shook the World*, and then produced *The General Line* (1929), called in the West *Old and New*. Needless to say, Eisenstein, who himself gave homage to Griffith, exercised an influence over all succeeding cinema.

End of the Avant-Garde in Europe

In 1929 the International Congress of Independent Film was held in La Sarraz, Switzerland. Eisenstein came, along with delegations from thirteen other countries. The Congress met again in November of 1930, and disbanded itself. This was notice of the fact that the first film avant-garde was over. The grim realities of the Depression were forcing film artists to become more socially and politically involved. Also, the arrival of the sound film had made silent films seem obsolete, and sound films were too expensive for experimentalists to make. Thus most members of the avant-garde either dropped film-making or made commercial documentaries or features.

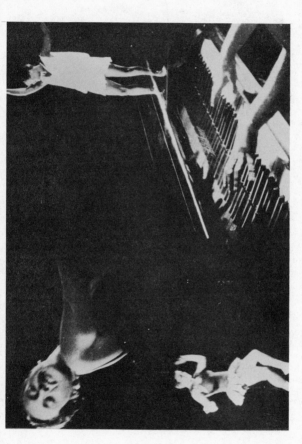

Vertov's *Man with a Camera* utilized the "trick" potential of the camera's eye. (*Collection Standish D. Lawder*)

George Hugnetos appeared in his *La Perle* (1931), made at the end of the avant-garde in Belgium. (*Collection Museum of Modern Art Film Library*)

America

The fireworks were almost over in Europe when the first film avant-garde started in America. An independent film was made as early as 1921. Charles Sheeler and Paul Strand's *Manhatta* (1921). But this documentary of New York City in long shots, with titles from a poem by Walt Whitman, is almost a series of static photographs, however well framed those photographs are. It caused no great excitement, and with the exception of another independent documentary on New York, also mainly long shots, Robert Flaherty's *24 Dollar Island* (1925), there was no independent activity. *Manhatta* was shown as a short in commercial theatres, and once in France on a dadaist program. *24 Dollar Island* was cut up to be used as background in a theatre for a live dance routine called "The Sidewalks of New York."

Then, in a series of small art houses around the country, the films from Europe and Russia began to appear. *The Cabinet of Doctor Caligari, Variety, The Last Laugh, Le Ballet Mécanique, La Chute de la Maison Usher, Emak Bakia, Man with a Camera*, and many others stirred a new interest in film as art, and even, in some cases, film as personal art. The three areas that had the most influence in forming the small American avant-garde were the German films with their expressionist sets, lighting, and acting, the Russian films with their editing, and the French avant-garde works with their trick techniques and sense of poetry.

The first independent production with experimental overtones appears to have been *The Last Moment* (1927), the work of Paul Fejos, who, before coming to America, had been a director of Hungarian films. It was the story of a drowning man who saw his life flashing by in front of him, and it opened and closed with rapid montages that summed up the content. It used the dissolves, multiple exposures, irises, split screens, and so on, that were by this time the official marks of an avant-garde film. *The Last Moment* was described as being expressionist, as was the less original *Tell-Tale Heart* (1928), based on Poe's story and directed by Charles Klein. Essentially a Hollywood production, *The Tell-Tale Heart* was considered avant-garde because it aped the style and sets of *Caligari*.

It was not until *The Life and Death of 9413—A Hollywood Extra* (1928) that anything like the spritely personal films of France were made in America. *A Hollywood Extra* was directed by Robert Florey, a Frenchman who had been working in the Hollywood studios, was designed by Slavko Vorkapich, and photographed by Gregg Toland. The film is a satire on Hollywood and a fantasy about a would-be star who cannot rise above the role of extra. It consists primarily of close-ups of faces and of miniature sets that were constructed on a table in Vorkapich's kitchen. Florey made two more experimental fantasies, *The Loves of Zero* (1929) and *Johann the Coffin Maker* (1929). *Zero* included shots with Zero's face split into two different-sized parts, and one with Zero walking home on Machine Street, while the upper portion of the screen is full of superimposed revolving machinery.

On the other side of the country, in Rochester, New York, a unique version of Poe's *The Fall of the House of Usher* (1928) was written by Melville Webber and photographed and directed by Dr. James Sibley Watson. It used shadows on wallboard (instead of sets), prismatic lenses, and a precise manipulation of form and light to tell the story in an intense and abstract way. Later Watson and Webber made *Lot in Sodom* (1933–34), again displaying remarkable precision in the control of movement and light. *Lot in Sodom* is a longer and more ambitious work than the first. It utilizes more actors and actresses to better effect, with lyric use of multiple exposures and distorting lenses, and with a sensuous sense of light, to tell the Old Testament story of a sinful city.

Ralph Steiner, a photographer in New York, made H_2O (1929), a classic study of the patterns of light and textures on the surface of water. It was an American version of the pattern film that had become so popular in Europe, and its success led Steiner to make two more pattern films, *Mechanical Principles* (1931), which took as its subject the movement of valves and gears, and *Surf and Seaweed* (1931). Herman G. Weinberg also followed the genres of the European avant-garde with his *City Symphony* (1929), after Ruttmann's *Berlin*, and his *Autumn Fire* (1930), a sentimental film poem after Kirsanov's *Brumes d'Automne*.

There was Jo Gercon and Hershell Louis's *The Story of a Nobody* (1930), which attempted to be entirely subjective,

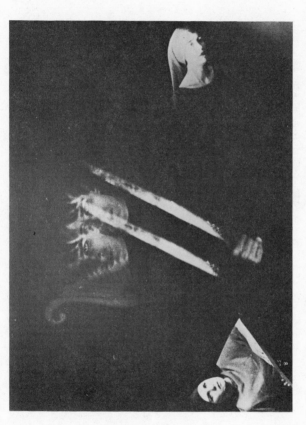

The Angel of God appears in this frame blowup from Watson and Webber's *Lot in Sodom*. (*Collection Museum of Modern Art Film Library*)

Ralph Steiner was already a renowned photographer when he made H_2O, his first film. (Collection Museum of Modern Art Film Library)

showing, according to Lewis Jacobs, "who they were, where they were, what they saw and did solely by objects." There was Charles Vidor's *The Spy* (1931–32), a film that, after Ambrose Bierce's "An Occurrence at Owl Creek Bridge," experimented with showing the getaway of a man imagined as the man is hanged.

As in Europe, the avant-garde in America essentially disappeared in 1931, leaving a string of poetic documentaries and socially conscious independent productions that surprised nobody and changed nothing. As in Europe, too, many experimentalists became successful in commercial work, including Fejos and Florey, who directed; Vorkapich, who was Hollywood's specialist in montage sequences; Steiner, who photographed documentaries; and Toland, who was the cinematographer on *Citizen Kane*.

The Depression

Few avant-garde films were made during the Depression.

Emlen Etting, a painter, made three film poems during this time, *Oramunde* (1931), *Poem 8* (1932), a romantic film in which the camera takes the place of the protagonist, and *Laureate* (1939). Roger Barlow, LeRoy Robbins, Harry Hay, and Hy Hirsch made a satire on surrealist films called *Even as You and I* (1937), which included one scene, reminiscent of the sliced eye in *Un Chien Andalou*, where a baby is laid on a plate, sliced up and served out for dinner. Ralph Steiner worked with Elia Kazan, Molly Day Thacher, and Irving Lerner to improvise *Pie in the Sky* (1934) in a city dump. John Flory and Theodore Huff made an experimental drama called *Mr. Motorboat's Last Stand* (1933). And there was an independent feature, called *Dawn to Dawn* (1934), written by Seymour Stern and directed by Joseph Berne. It is about a lonely farm girl who falls in love with an itinerant laborer, and is very naturalistic in approach.

Lewis Jacobs was involved in a number of projects, including *Commercial Medley*, which was a take-off on film previews of coming attractions; *Underground Printer*, a political satire dance film; and *Synchronization* (1934), an animated work done with Joseph Schillinger and Mary Ellen Bute.

When Oskar Fischinger arrived in America from Germany,

Emlen Etting's *Oramunde* was one of the first personal films in America to be made by a painter.

he continued with his absolute films animated to music. He produced *Allegretto* (1936), *Optical Poem* (1937) for MGM, *An American March* (1939), and, later, *Motion Painting No. 1* (1949), an animated oil painting on glass. Both Fischinger's work and his actual presence were stimuli that helped set off the second film avant-garde.

Mary Ellen Bute, who had first worked with Lewis Jacobs, now produced a long series of animated films with her husband Ted Nemeth. These films included *Rhythm in Light* (1936), *Synchrony No. 2* (1936), *Parabola* (1938), *Escape* (1940), *Tarantella* (1941), *Polka-Graph* (1953), *Abstronics* (1954), *Color Rhapsody* (1954), and *Mood Contrast* (1954), the later films using electronic imagery and oscillo-scope-generated images. Bute's live-action films include the short *The Boy Who Saw Through* (1956–58), an experimental feature based on Joyce's *Finnegans Wake* (1964–65), and most recently a version of Wilder's *The Skin of Our Teeth* (1966–   ). Many of the abstract works, made in 35mm, were sold to Radio City Music Hall in New York City for showing there.

Douglas Crockwell, a commercial advertising and story illustrator, made abstract films that were time paintings. He placed a camera over a glass table, and recorded with it the form and color evolutions he painted or scraped away on the glass. He started with simple compositions in *Fantasmagoria I* (1938), and eventually produced what appeared to be complex plastic landscapes in *Glen Falls Sequence* (1946) and *The Long Bodies* (1946–47). *The Long Bodies* utilized a technique whereby cross-sections of varicolored wax blocks were photographed as they were sliced away, one frame per thin slice, producing an animation of color patterns flowing in the wax. In 1949 Crockwell began working with Muto-scopes, the old penny-arcade flip-card machines that slightly predated motion picture projectors. Since that time he has redesigned the basic Mutoscope, and has created a number of abstract works for viewing on it.

Lye and McLaren in England

During this period there were two men working in England who later had an effect on avant-garde film in America. One was Len Lye, and the other was Norman McLaren.

Lye was a native of New Zealand and the first man to draw the whole film directly on the film stock itself. As a young artist he went to Australia to learn film animation, and as early as 1921 he was experimenting with scratching dynamic forms on the film surface. Later he went to England. After making *Tusalava* (1928), a photographed animation film, he experimented with painting on film, because the only film stock he could afford was clear film, cadged off friends in the professional studios. The result got him a job with John Grierson's G.P.O. Film Unit, itself best known for documentaries such as *Night Mail* and *Song of Ceylon*. At G.P.O. Lye made *Colour Box* (1935), which led to more films for both the government and private advertisers. These included *Kaleidoscope* (1935), *The Birth of the Robot* (1936), *Rainbow Dance* (1936), *Trade Tatoo* (1937), *Swinging the Lambeth Walk* (1939), and *Musical Poster* (1940). Each film used new techniques, many combining live action with animated materials in jumpy rhythms and brilliant colors. A work such as *Trade Tatoo* has yet to be matched for technical resourcefulness.

After the war, Lye came to the United States. Having made war effort documentaries in England, he worked in New York for *The March of Time* series. On his own he produced *Color Cry* (1952), *Rhythm* (1953), and then *Free Radicals* (1958), which was entirely made of animating lines scratched into the film surface. He publicly announced his withdrawal from the film medium, because of lack of support, and became a leading kinetic sculptor. Secretly, however, he spent five years producing another scratch-film work, *Particles in Space* (1961–66).

McLaren, from Scotland, had already made a trick-technique film, *Camera Makes Woopee* (1935) and had tried to draw on film (after seeing one of Oskar Fischinger's films), before he made his first abstract work, *Colour Cocktail* (1935). He was evidently much influenced by Lye's *Colour Box* and worked in the room next to Lye's at G.P.O. Since that time he has become one of the world's most influential animators. As Lye was probably the first to draw the image directly on the film, McLaren was probably the first, with *Allegro* (1939), to *draw* the sound track directly on the film. His films number over fifty, some of them being pixilated live action, such as the famous *Neighbors* (1952);

some of them being abstract, such as the recent *Mosaic* (1965). Although his works are always sponsored, McLaren is within the tradition of the personal film artist. Having moved to the United States in 1939, and then to Canada in 1941, he now works for the Canadian Film Board, where he is given the freedom to make whatever films he wishes.

Second Film Avant-Garde

The second film avant-garde began as the Depression ended. Sixteen-millimeter film and equipment, available since 1923, were becoming more accessible, and the Second World War, because its training films and features for the troops were on 16mm, rapidly increased this accessibility. Sixteen-millimeter was less expensive than 35mm, the film stock used by the first avant-garde, and the coming of prosperity eased the money problem in this expensive art medium.

There was, too, the effect of the Museum of Modern Art's circulating film programs, starting in 1937, which brought back into sight the refreshing old French trick films and the work of the first avant-garde. Later the Art in Cinema showings in San Francisco and those of Cinema 16 in New York gave publicity to the personal art film and a chance for exhibition to the new film-makers.

By 1941 Crockwell, Bute, and Nemeth and some new people were already at work. Francis Lee made *1941*, an abstract antiwar film. He was then drafted and left the pawn ticket for his camera in the hands of Marie Menken and Willard Maas, soon to become film-makers themselves. Dwinnel Grant made *Themis* (1940), *Contrathemis* (1941), and *Three Dimensional Experiments* (1945), all abstract films. Mylon Meriam made unnamed abstract films (1941–42). And Christopher Young made *Object Lesson* (1941), a work that employed symbolic objects placed in natural environments to give the effect of a journey through a sur-realist landscape. His later *Subject Lesson* (1953–55) did much the same thing in color.

The West Coast Revival

It was in 1943, however, on the West Coast that the avant-garde film, then called the experimental film, began its real comeback. The second film avant-garde lasted approximately from 1943 to 1954. The work that set the dominant style in live action for that period was Maya Deren and Alexander Hammid's *Meshes of the Afternoon* (1943).

Meshes of the Afternoon is a surrealist nightmare film. It has a sense of terror and of psychological abnormality. The story concerns a girl who becomes shaken by a series of small incidents, including a figure disappearing around the curve of the road, a key dropping, and a large knife found on a table. The environment of the house then appears to rock back and forth, throwing the girl about; the figure who disappears around the curve is seen to have a mirror face; and the knife appears everywhere until the girl, evidently, kills herself with it. Deren and Hammid acted in and photographed the film in Los Angeles. Hammid, a well-known maker of documentaries who had come from Europe, whose original name was Hackenschmied, was married to Deren at the time.

Maya Deren made the rest of her films in New York, the next being *At Land* (1944), in which a girl, again Deren, is born of the sea, adventures through "life," and returns to the sea. In one of its most memorable scenes she crawls on her stomach down the middle of a banquet table with people dining on both sides. *A Study in Choreography for Camera* (1945) is a presentation of a dancer, Talley Beatty, dancing in a camera-created space and time. A leap starts in a wood and lands in a room. A pirouette starts in a room and ends in a gallery at the Metropolitan Museum of Art, and so on. *Ritual in Transfigured Time* (1946) is a dance drama, and both *Meditation on Violence* (1948) and *The Very Eye of Night* (1959) involve dance. *Meditation on Violence* uses the movements of a Chinese boxer, but manipulates them with the camera, through backwards and slow motion, into a dance. *The Very Eye of Night* transforms choreographed dancers, with negative footage and a moving camera, into dreamy constellations gliding effortlessly across the frame. Unfinished films by Deren include a work on Haitian voodoo and *The Witch's Cradle*, with Marcel Duchamp acting, photographed at the surrealist *Art of this Century* gallery. She died in 1961.

In Los Angeles, where *Meshes* had been made, three more film-makers emerged, Kenneth Anger, Curtis Harrington, and

Maya Deren, herself, played the central character in *Meshes of the Afternoon*. (*Collection* Film Culture)

The dancers in Deren's *The Very Eye of Night* seem to have transcended gravity and reality. (*Collection* Film Culture)

Gregory Markopoulos. All three had made films as children. All three made works that were obviously very personal. All three made works that were almost confessions.

Kenneth Anger had been a child actor in Hollywood movies, and made his own first film in 1941. His first exhibited film was *Escape Episode* (1944–46), and soon after that, while he was still in high school, he made *Fireworks* (1947), a notorious work about sado-masochistic homosexuality. In the film a boy, played by Anger, is spectacularly beaten up by sailors. His heart is torn from his entrails and revealed to be an electric meter. And when the penis of a sailor becomes a shooting roman candle, Anger turns into a tinsel-laden Christmas tree in ironic ecstasy.

Also working on the theme of attraction "between the same sex" was Gregory Markopoulos. His first work to gain attention was *Psyche* (1947–48), which used a fragmentary editing technique that obliterated the plot if one did not know it. The film ends with a montage summary of the key scenes, somewhat like the ending of Fejos's *The Last Moment*. *Psyche* was the first film of a trilogy, *Du Sang de la Volupté et de la Mort*. In *Lysis* (1948) Markopoulos himself appears in a memoir of objects and scenes, and *Charmides* (1948) completes the trilogy. The editing style introduced in *Psyche* was continued with *Swain* (1951) and has become increasingly complex in Markopoulos's later films.

Across the hall from Markopoulos lived Curtis Harrington, who was at the time a close friend of Kenneth Anger. Harrington had made three films in 8mm, including a version of *The Fall of the House of Usher*, before he made, in 16mm, *Fragment of Seeking* (1946). Concerned with the myth of Narcissus, and originally titled *Symbol of Decadence*, the key image in this film appears in a scene in which the hero, played by Harrington, finally works up the nerve to embrace a girl. Then it is revealed that the girl is a skeleton wearing a wig. Harrington made *Picnic* (1948), *On the Edge* (1949), *Dangerous Houses* (1952), *The Assignation* (1953), and a film about the paintings of a mystic named Cameron, *The Wormwood Star* (1955). The most often seen of these is *On the Edge*, a strongly symbolic work in which a man grabs a ball of yarn from a knitting woman and runs with it down a road into a bubbling crater of mud.

Harrington became a director of commercial features,

mostly horror films. Both Markopoulos and Anger continued to make personal works.

San Francisco developed its own film ferment. Sidney Peterson and James Broughton together made *The Potted Psalm* (1946), a wildly disorganized collection of surrealistic sight gags. After this Peterson began teaching a course in film-making, called Workshop 20, at the California School of Fine Arts, and there produced a number of films, including *The Cage* (1947) about a runaway eyeball, *The Petrified Dog* (1948), *Mr. Frenhofer and the Minotaur* (1949), and *The Lead Shoes* (1949). *The Lead Shoes* is perhaps the most successful of these; it is the story of a mother who is trying to rescue her son, who is somehow dead in a diving suit. The action is alternately squeezed and stretched by an anamorphic lens, and two scrambled ballads are chanted and sung in accompaniment to the scrambled pictures. (After Peterson ceased personal film work, he gave this distorting lens to Stan Brakhage, who is still using it.)

James Broughton, a poet, produced a series of satirical works: the perverse *Mother's Day* (1948), in which adults act like children; *The Adventures of Jimmy* (1950), which is a humorous and purposely naive autobiography; *Four in the Afternoon* (1951) about four searches for love; and *Loony Tom* (1951), a take-off on the old comedies of Charlie Chaplin. Broughton's last film to be released was *The Pleasure Garden* (1953).

Many people dabbled in personal film-making on the West Coast. Joseph Vogel, a painter, made *House of Cards* (1947) and *All the News* (1947), both stylized psychodramas. Chester Kessler, who had helped with the camera work on *Fireworks*, made a one-of-a-kind film, *Plague Summer* (1951), which employed crude drawings to accompany a reading from Kenneth Patchen's allegorical "The Journal of Albion Moonlight." Weldon Kees, a trumpeter who did sound tracks for many San Francisco films, made a strange exploration of a ruined structure in *Hotel Apex* (1952). Richard S. Brummer made *The Drum* (1952) and *First Fear* (1952).

In New York a limited resurgence accompanied the West Coast activity. Willard Maas, with the technical aid of his wife, Marie Menken, made *Geography of the Body* (1943), a *tour de force* that used dime-store magnifying lenses to

The main character of Peterson's *The Cage* periodically lost one of his eyeballs in this film produced in San Francisco. (*Collection Museum of Modern Art Film Library*)

make horrifying close-ups of various parts of the human body. This was followed by *Images in the Snow* (1943–48), another psychodrama about an alienated homosexual. *The Mechanics of Love* (1955), made by Maas with Ben Moore, was a compilation of Freudian symbols for various parts of making love. And Moore and Maas made another alienated homosexual film, *Narcissus* (1956), starring Moore. Marie Menken also made a film during this period, a dynamic study of sculpture called *Visual Variations on Noguchi* (1945), which was the prelude to a later and very prolific career as a personal film-maker.

Hans Richter, in New York because of the Nazi take-over in Europe, discovered that other expatriot artist friends were also in New York and decided to do a film with them. Alexander Calder, Marcel Duchamp, Max Ernst, Fernand Léger, and Man Ray wrote scenarios that Richter directed in a framework of his own making. The result, the widely publicized *Dreams That Money Can Buy* (1944–46), feature length and in color, was less than the masterpiece that his earlier films had been. Because it was acted in by prominent members of the art world, however, *Dreams* became something of an addition to art history. The same was true of his second experimental feature, *8 x 8* (1957), which used many of the same people, plus Jean Cocteau.

Robert Vickrey, an artist, also made experimental narratives. These included *Texture of Decay* (1947–53), about a man driven to suicide by the atmosphere of an abandoned house; *Oedipus* (1950–53), a retelling of the myth in more symbolic terms; and *Appointment with Darkness* (1950–53) about a girl contemplating self-destruction. In a lighter vein, Vickrey made *Carnival* (1950–53), *Miracle for Sale Cheap* (1956), a later version of *Miracle* called *Ellen in Window Land* (1956–57), and *Playground* (1957).

Ian Hugo made brilliantly colored works in which the action is suffused with many superimpositions that yield abstract compositions. His first film was *Ai-Ye* (1950) and was followed by *Bells of Atlantis* (1952). *Bells of Atlantis* was inspired by "House of Incest," a poem by Anais Nin, Hugo's wife. It starred Nin, and with a technical assist from Len Lye and electronic sound by Louis and Bebe Barron, it gave an imaginary look at life in the sunken city of Atlantis. Later Hugo made *Jazz of Lights* (1954) of lights in Times

Square, *Melodic Inversion* (1958), and two film poems about
Venice, *Venice Etude No. 1* (1962) and *The Gondola Eye*
(1963).

Dance and Pattern Films

Allied to the psychodramas were the dance films. Deren
set the style with *A Study in Choreography for Camera*,
which showed dance, but with the element of cinematic
control added to poetic effect.

Sarah Arledge's *Introspection* (1947), for example, used
extreme distorting lenses and dancers in costumes with
certain parts blacked out so that only certain movements
showed. Sidney Peterson made *Horror Dream* (1947) and
Clinic of Stumble (1947). Yael Woll made *Study of a Dance*
about "two lovers trapped and helpless in the tempo and
awesomeness of their time." Shirley Clarke stopped dancing
to make dance films, including *Dance in the Sun* (1953),
Bullfight (1955), and *A Moment in Love* (1957). Her
Bridges-Go-Round (1958–59), produced before she became
a director in independent features, is a superimpositional
"dance" of New York bridges.

As in the first film avant-garde, large numbers of works
used common objects as abstract elements in a film design.
These works include Dorsey Alexander's stop-motion animated *Life and Death of a Sphere* (1948) and *Dime Store*
(1949), Jose Pavone's *Forms in Motion*, and Ernest Beadle's
Myself When Young, apparently an autobiography suggested
by objects. Francis Lee used costume jewelry and stop-
motion photography to make *Le Bijou* (1947) and also *The
Idyl* (1948). *Proem* (1949) by Leonard Tregillus and R. W.
Luce, and the better-known *Gumbasia* (1955) by Art Clokey
both used clay manipulated through various effects with
stop-motion.

Also somewhat like the pattern films of the first avant-
garde are the works of Wheaton Gelentine. His *Water Stars*
(1952) is reminiscent of Steiner's H_2O. And his *Treadle and
Bobbin* (1954) is a modern version of Eugene Deslaw's
Marche des Machines, the subject matter in this case being
restricted to a sewing machine.

There were, too, a number of city symphonies. Frank
Stauffacher made *Sausilito* (1948) about that city, *Zig Zag*

Francis Thompson turned a solid city into whimsical shapes in the startling *N.Y., N.Y.* (*Collection Museum of Modern Art Film Library*)

(1948) about neon lights, and *Notes on the Port of St. Francis* (1952), showing San Francisco. Philip Leff's *Symphony* (1951), John Arvonio's *Abstract in Concrete* and Allen Downs's *Freight Stop* (1954) are all versions of this genre. The most spectacularly experimental and successful of such films is Francis Thompson's *N.Y., N.Y.* (1957), in which a variety of distorting lenses were used to transform New York City into a series of plastic shapes.

Charles Eames, an architect and a designer, and his wife Ray, a painter, began making personal films during this period. Among the earliest were *Blacktop* (1950), a study of spreading water and the reflections made when the blacktop surface of a playground was being cleaned, *Parade* (1950); a parade of toys, *House* (1955), a portrait of their home in the form of a series of carefully composed stills; *Toccata for Toy Trains* (1957), a whole world created around toy trains; and *Kaleidoscope* (1961), a look around the Eames studios through a kaleidoscope. The Eameses, with their design staff, have made over thirty films to date, many of them commissioned by organizations like Herman Miller Furniture and I.B.M. They have also executed a number of pioneering multi-screen productions. All Eames films, single or multi-screen, personal or commissioned, have a sense of precise design and visual richness.

The West Coast Abstract School

Several years before Deren and Hammid made *Meshes of the Afternoon*, there began on the West Coast a school of abstract film-making that has remained fairly isolated and unique. The members of this school, James and John Whitney, Harry Smith, and Jordan Belson, took as their starting place the works of Eggeling, Richter, and Fischinger, and went on to develop a new set of forms and techniques.

John Whitney, a film-maker and technical innovator, and his brother James Whitney, a painter, began experimenting with a series of abstract film forms, animated on cards, called *Variations* (1941–43). They were involved in working with relationships between film and music. The Whitneys, however, felt that the use of conventional music would limit, because of the associations of memory, the imaginative responses of the audience, and therefore they developed a machine that could produce electronic music directly on the sound track of the film, and in perfect synchronization with the images.

The images of the Whitneys' *Film Exercises*, produced with paper cut-outs, a modified optical printer, pantographs, and color filters, were hard-edge forms that in succeeding works became increasingly intense in color and movement. The first work to have the specially composed electronic sound track was *Film Exercise 1* (1943). *Exercises 2* and *3* (1944) were fragments of never finished works that led to the highly accomplished *Film Exercises 4* and *5* (1944).

At this point the two brothers began to work separately. John Whitney developed a way to make abstract films without animation: the setting up of an oil bath that let light through to be photographed only where the oil was displaced by a stylus. Using this method, and in some cases using hand-manipulated paper cut-outs, he made many films to specific songs, among them *Mozart Rondo* (1947–49), *Hot House* (1947–49), *Celery Stalks at Midnight* (1951), and a color version of *Celery Stalks at Midnight* (1957). Later he hooked up an optical printer to a war surplus analog computer to produce exceedingly complex effects that were used primarily for television program and feature-film titles. An informal selection of these effects was put together in *Catalogue* (1961).

James Whitney developed a series of equally complex animation techniques. Using some of them, he made *Yantra* (1950–55), which showed continually flowing material in a series of pulsating motions. By its title *Yantra* appears to be meant as an instrument of Hindu contemplation and worship. *Lapis* (1963–66) was made with a computer similar to the one used by his brother.

While the Whitneys worked in Los Angeles, Harry Smith was in San Francisco reinventing the process of painting directly on film. (He was disturbed when he found out later that Len Lye had already made such films in the early thirties.) Smith animated his absolute films to 4/4 time, adding whatever music seemed appropriate, most recently The Beatles. In his first film, which he dates 1939, but which may have been finished as late as 1947, the forms are abstractly organic and rather sexual. Later he produced more complex works with dancing circles, designs in batik,

and op-art squares. After 1949 he worked with optical printing, producing, among others, a three-dimensional film,
Number 6 (1951). In 1954 he switched to animated collages,
leaving abstract film-making; he is now working in the field
of live-action film.

The Whitney films, shown along with those of Richter and
Fischinger at the first Art in Cinema series in San Francisco,
induced Jordan Belson, a painter, to begin abstract film-
making. Starting with *Transmutation* (1947), his early films
used mainly stop-motion techniques, which he later abandoned for continual action and the manipulation of light.
These new techniques and materials, used in *Allures* (1960),
for example, were so much more satisfying to Belson that he
has destroyed the negatives of early works.

These four were the innovators but not the only members
of the West Coast abstract school. Hy Hirsch, a photographer
who helped with the camera work on a number of experimental films, made his own films, often using oscilloscope
patterns printed through color filters and superimposed on
one another. Films by Hirsch, who died in Europe in 1960,
include *Autumn Spectrum, Chasse des Toches, Come Closer,
Défense d'Afficher, Divertissement Rococo* (1952); *Double
Jam, Eneri, Gyromorphosis* (1958); *Mad Nest, Recherche,*
and *Scratch Pad.*

Patricia Marx shows the influence of Harry Smith in
Obmaru (1953) and *Things To Come* (1953). And Jane
Conger, Belson's wife at one time, made *Logos* (1957) and
the unorganized *Odds and Ends.*

Many of the West Coast group were involved in the
historical *Vortex Concerts* (1957–59), predecessors of "expanded cinema." The *Vortex Concerts* were started by Henry
Jacobs, an electronic composer, who acquired the use of the
Morrison Planetarium at the California Academy of Sciences
in San Francisco to give environmental concerts of modern
music. The planetarium had complete soundproofing, total
blackness, a fifty-speaker sound system, and it seated five
hundred people. The initial sound concerts were soon bol-
stered by the manipulation of light, and after the second
series, Jordan Belson became the visual director of the
concerts.

The *Vortex Concerts* used up to seventy projectors to provide a variety of special effects, designs on rotating slides

that seemed to float in space, moire-type interference patterns that covered the dome, and stroboscopic phenomena. The later concerts included film footage by James Whitney, Jordan Belson, and Hy Hirsch. Each concert was carefully programmed and rehearsed for a fifty-minute performance; a total of sixty-two performances were given in all. The fifth of the series of six was presented at the Brussels World's Fair in 1958. The *Vortex Concerts* ended when the unique facilities of the planetarium were withdrawn; the same personnel gave visual presentations in less spectacular environments for several years after that.

Other Abstract Work

On the East Coast there was no given school of abstract work. The only Eastern film-maker to produce a significant number of abstract films was James Davis. Davis, a painter, worked with illuminated plastics and with light and colors reflected off irregularly shaped plastic surfaces. His films include *Painting and Plastics* (1948), *Shadows and Light Reflections* (1948), *Light Reflections* (1948), *Color and Light No. 1* (1950), *Reflections No. 11* (1951), *Refractions No. 1* (1951), *Color Dances No. 1* (1952), *Analogies No. 1* (1953), *Thru the Looking Glass* (1954), *Becoming* (1955), *Evolutions* (1955), *Writ in Water* (1955), *Energies* (1957), *Death and Transfiguration* (1961–65), and *Impulses* (1965). Davis also produced a series of documentaries on the painter John Marin and on Frank Lloyd Wright.

A number of other people made one or two abstract films during this time, including Hugo Latelin with *Color Designs # 1* (1948), Robert Howard with *Meta* (1947), and Hal McCormick with *Suite # 2* (1947). Roger Bruce Rogers made *Toccata Manhatta* (1949), *Rhapsody Motion Painting III* (1951), *Appassionata Fantasy,* plus an animated work that traced the style of painting through its stages, *Round Trip in Modern Art* (1949).

End of the Second Film Avant-Garde

Films produced in the second avant-garde differed from those produced in the first in that they were more personal and less commercial. The film-makers worked on 16mm, not 35mm, and they financed their films themselves.

Yet while the experimental films were made with integrity, many of them lacked vitality. Their emphasis was on other arts, and they tended to be, though more involved with cinematic means, as literary, as static, and as limited as the commercial films from which they had set themselves apart. Their initial premises and their resulting forms were not so very new, and in the end, many film-makers, their interest, energy, and finances exhausted, found themselves in a *cul-de-sac*. The second avant-garde as a movement ended around 1954. The more talented individuals, Anger, Markopoulos, Whitney, Smith, Belson, and so on, continued to produce important films, and twenty years later are producing them still.

The Forming of the Underground Avant-Garde

There was, as the second avant-garde disappeared, a whole new group of people beginning to make films. They were located in Paris, New York, Connecticut, Wichita, Denver, and San Francisco. There was not any consistency in their emergence. A number of different kinds of young artists began to use the film medium to express themselves. They worked alone, with improvised equipment, and as they went along, their equipment got better, their films got better, and they began to know each other.

In 1952 Robert Breer started filming while still in Paris. In 1953 Jonas Mekas, Christopher MacLaine, and Stan Brakhage finished first films. In 1954 it was Larry Jordan, the Kuchar brothers, Carmen D'Avino, and Stan VanDer-Beek. In 1956 it was Ken Jacobs and Jack Smith. Marie Menken returned to film in 1957, and Joseph Marzano and George Manupelli started. Robert Branaman, Bruce Conner, and Richard Preston began in 1958. In 1959 Ed Emshwiller finished his first film, and in 1960 it was Ron Rice, Vernon Zimmerman, and Bruce Baillie. These people, along with the people who were still going strong from the experimental period, made up the first generation of the underground film-makers.

The formality and sense of nightmarish despair that had

pervaded the experimental psychodramas gave way, in the new works, to a sense of flow and lyricism. In the films of Christopher MacLaine, for example, a pre-underground film-maker, the neurotic gloom of *The End* (1953) was replaced by the freer and more spontaneous *The Man Who Invented Gold, Scotch Hop*, and *Beat*. This same transition is visible in the films of Brakhage. The tightness and terror of *Reflections on Black* (1955) dissolves into the freeness and beauty of *The Wonder Ring* (1955). The concern with myth and archetype in the first becomes the concern with light and with seeing in the second.

Even in one of Brakhage's earliest films, a story of a teen-age party that gets out of hand called *Desistfilm* (1954), one can find certain characteristics of the new avant-garde. There is an awareness of film as material and as arbitrator of light, as revealed by the titles scratched into the film itself (and in the scratches over the blind man's eyes in *Reflections on Black*). There is an uncommon identification between the eye of the camera and the eye of the film-maker. The camera movement in *Desistfilm* is almost as if the camera were something alive. And there is a nervous vitality communicated both by the camera movement and by the rapid cutting.

The films of the second avant-garde, being based on literature, or drama, or poetry, or dance, looked like official art. The new films were not so easily identifiable. There were film portraits, mementoes, visual essays, personal documentaries, and many films that didn't have genres.

Robert Breer made a film in which each frame was an entirely different shot, *Image by Images I* (1954). Marie Menken made a film composed entirely of bumping dollies through a garden accompanied by a sound track of "canned canaries." Stan Brakhage made a film on masturbation, *Flesh of Morning* (1956–57), later *Anticipation of the Night* (1958) in which he tried, by complete fragmentation, to show vision without preconception, and afterwards *Window Water Baby Moving* (1959), a no-holds-barred look at his first child being born. In *A Movie* (1958) Bruce Conner took old newsreel footage and glued it together in a new way to make a film poem. Bob Branaman was putting film in an 8mm camera and shooting, and rewinding, and pointing the camera at other things, and shooting again with the same film to produce his "rolls." The Kuchar Brothers, teen-age twins, were making 8mm Hollywood movie take-offs such as *I Was a Teen Age Rumpot* (1958).

An important factor contributing to the growth of the underground was the tide of dissent that was stirring through the country. This involved the passive and not so passive nonconformity of the Beats, the discontent with the "normal" way of living, and attempts to develop points of view other than those of Western civilization. This was a move toward liberation, a move toward a sense of a new kind of man. The introduction of hallucinogenic drugs was part of this attempt, and so was the push towards sexual freedom. All these elements were reflected in the films being made by individuals. And the films themselves were part of this dissent.

There were, too, the happenings in the world of cinema. The works of the first avant-garde were still being circulated by the Museum of Modern Art, and were still working their magic. The films of the second avant-garde were being distributed by Cinema 16 and other sources. There were the films from Post-War Europe, the Italian neorealist works and Cocteau's surrealist fantasies. And from England, in the late fifties, came news of a revolt by young film-makers against the stodgy films of the establishment. The revolt was called "Free Cinema," and it took the form of documentaries such as *Momma Don't Allow* (1956) by Karel Reisz and Tony Richardson, and *Every Day Except Christmas* (1957) by Lindsay Anderson. These films did not have much effect in America, but the idea of a formal revolt did.

The arrival of the New Wave films from France, the so-called art films of Bergman, Fellini, Antonioni, Wadja, Kurosawa, and so on, helped shake the situation even more. Europe also provided an experimental film festival, in Brussels, in 1958. (When the awards were given out, the Americans were well represented, by people like Brakhage, Hirsch, Anger, Hilary Harris, and Len Lye.)

On the home front, the New York School of film-makers was producing less commercial, hence low-budget narratives. This trend started with Sidney Myers's *The Quiet One* (1948) and with the work of Morris Engel. He made *The Little Fugitive* (1953), *Lovers and Lollipops* (1956), and *Weddings and Babies* (1956) with portable equipment and small crews on location. Lionel Rogosin made *On the Bowery*

(1957), a documentary with a story injected, and later *Come Back Africa* (1959), a film about the problems of the Negroes in South Africa, again with a story injected. Alfred Leslie wrote and directed and Robert Frank photographed a dramatic short, *Pull My Daisy* (1958), a very fluid work (based on the third act of a play by Jack Kerouac called *The Beat Generation*) that appeared improvised but was actually carefully rehearsed. John Cassavetes, working with a group to whom he was teaching film-making, made for under $15,000 a feature called *Shadows* (1957). Later additions to the New York School were Shirley Clarke with *The Connection* (1960) and *The Cool World* (1963), Robert Frank as a director with *The Sin of Jesus* (1961), and Bert Stern with the free-wheeling color documentary *Jazz on a Summer's Day* (1961).

The New American Cinema

The New York School of film-makers, though more cinematically conservative than the members of the developing underground, had the same problems as the underground. They couldn't get financing to make the films they wanted to, and they couldn't get satisfactory distribution when they did manage to make films. Thus the two independent elements came together to deal with these problems. On September 28, 1960, a number of film-makers met at the New York office of producer Lewis Allen to found what they called "The New American Cinema Group." In their first statement, they rejected censorship, declared film to be "indivisably a personal expression," and set up plans for cooperative financing and distribution. The statement ended with these words: "We don't want false, polished, slick films—we prefer them rough, unpolished, but alive; we don't want rosy films—we want them the color of blood."

The more commercially minded members of the group tried to continue within the framework of commercial distribution. The avant-garde film-makers, having little choice, started working with the ideas propounded, and a year and a half later, in 1962, the Film-makers' Cooperative was founded. The man who masterminded it was Jonas Mekas, publisher of *Film Culture*, director of the experimental feature *Guns of the Trees* (1960–61), the same man who had brought together the semicommercial and avant-garde elements to set up the New American Cinema Group. Under his leadership, the Film-makers' Cooperative adopted a policy of distributing all films submitted to it, with nobody ruling as to their quality. This was in line with the attitude of the emerging avant-garde that it was the film artists who knew what ought to be seen, not the distributors, not the exhibitors, and not the audience. Following this idea, a series of film showcases, operated by the film-makers, were set up to insure minimal exhibition.

The Third Film Avant-Garde

There were, then, all these people in separate parts of the country making films. They started making films in the early fifties, and by the beginning of the sixties it was apparent that there existed a movement of considerable breadth.

The works of the third avant-garde were exceedingly intricate, with much rapid cutting, disparate continuity, and mobile hand-held photography. The films were self-consciously *film*. As in modern art, the materials and the processes of making the work of art (the grain, the scratching on film, the mid-frame splices, the shakey camera) became part of the work of art. The film-makers were not interested in creating a fictional reality for the camera to record objectively. Primarily they wanted to manipulate reality with camera and editing and to produce thereby a different, a film reality that had a sense of being film.

The third avant-garde films were mostly made with amateur equipment. They were more intimate, were, many of them, almost home movies. Some were horrifying and purposely abrasive home movies, like Jack Smith's *Flaming Creatures* (1962–63). But they were all primarily personal, personal expression, personal works of art.

Whereas the members of the first two avant-gardes usually made a limited number of personal films before going on to commercial films or out of the medium, underground film-makers tended to stick with the medium and with the mode of expression. As a painter would continue to paint paintings, the film-maker continued to film films.

The underground began to get publicity in 1961, mainly because certain people, who were taking up the cause of the personal art film, were writing about it and were putting on showings. These people included Mekas in New York, George Manupelli in Ann Arbor, Bruce Baillie in San Francisco, and John Fles in Los Angeles. All except Fles were film-makers.

Then there was an explosion in personal art film-making. It is too early to measure the magnitude of that explosion, although many of the second and third generations of underground film-makers are becoming known.

There was Andy Warhol, for example, with his now famous motionless movies. Red Grooms made *Shoot the Moon* (1962) and *Lurk* (1964) with Rudy Burckhardt, and by himself a series including *The Unwelcome Guests* (1961), *Man or Mouse* (1964), *Washington's Wig Wham* (1966), and *Fat Feet* (1966). Peter Goldman made *Echoes of Silence* (1962–65). Nathaniel Dorsky made a series of restrained and beautiful film poems culminating in *Summerwind* (1966). Storm de Hirsch made the mysterious shorts *Divinations* (1965) and *Peyote Queen* (1965), and a narrative feature called *Goodbye in the Mirror* (1964). Bill Vehr made flowery and perverse atmosphere films, including *Avocada* (1965) and *Brothel* (1966). Andrew Meyer made an ornate and intricately constructed version of *The Poor Little Match Girl* (1965). George Landow made the multiframe experimental portrait *Fleming Faloon* (1963–64).

On the West Coast there was almost a separate ferment, mainly centered around the Canyon Cinema group, which Bruce Baillie had founded. Carl Linder was working with intricate close-ups and demonic intent, producing such works as *The Devil Is Dead* (1964) and *Skin* (1965). Stanton Kaye made the supra-realistic *Georg* (1962–64). Ben Van Meter made *The Poontang Trilogy* (1964) and a series of psychedelic extravaganzas, including *Color Film* (1966) and *Up Tight, L.A. Is Burning . . . Shit* (1966). Robert Nelson made the galloping satire on racial problems *Oh Dem Watermelons* (1965) with the San Francisco Mime Troupe.

And there was an enormous number of film-makers who had personal works in distribution. Among them were Bob Chatterton, Bob Cowan, Lawrence Marinelli, Robert Downey, George Binkey, Raymond Saroff, Tony Siani, Ray

Wisniewski, Naomi Levine, Paul Morrisey, Barbara Rubin, Dick Higgins, Arnold Gassan, Bob Fleischner, William Earle, Gene Friedman, Clark Kent, Richard Myers, Ronald Nameth, Dennis Morgan, William Hindle, Barry Gerson, Dov Lederberg, Herb de Grasse, Joyce Weiland, Greg Barrios, Bhob Stewart, Daniel Howard, George Kling, Jud Yalkut, Stephan Lovi, Abbot Meader, Paul J. Sharits, José Rodriguez-Soltero, Charles Levine, David Brooks, Paul Beattie, Robert Feldman, Andrew Noren, Dave Bienstock, Cynthia Smagula, Earl Bodien, Allen Schaaf, Michael Midke, Lawrence Janiak, Al Saxton, John Hawkins, David Wise, Warren Sonbert, Piero Heliczer, Jerry Joffen, Lloyd Williams, Lennie Lipton, Sy Marcuse, Jerry Abrams, Lawrence Booth, Pat Oberhaus, William B. Hatfield, Loren Rehbock, Michael Wiese, Gerard Malanga, John Cavanaugh, and Gordon Ball. Not all these people were beginners, by any means. (Jerry Joffen, for example, is known to have influenced the work of such people as Ron Rice. He does not, however, exhibit his films, and is rumored to destroy his films almost as soon as he makes them.)

As the work of new film-makers began to appear, the older members of the underground were producing some of their best work. Stan Brakhage was making the epic *Dog Star Man* (1959–64). Gregory Markopoulos was making *Twice a Man* (1962–63). Bruce Baillie did *Mass* (1963–64) and *Quixote* (1964–65). Stan VanDerBeek made *Breathdeath* (1964). Jordan Belson made *Re-Entry* (1964). Jonas Mekas photographed *The Brig* (1964). Robert Breer made *Breathing* (1963) and *Fist Fight* (1964), Ed Emshwiller *Thanatopsis* (1960–62) and *Relativity* (1963–66), Larry Jordan *Duo Concertantes* (1962–64), and so on. This was a time in which previously developed techniques and sensibilities were being used to produce more refined works. Even Jack Smith followed his wild, censor-rousing *Flaming Creatures* (1962–63) with the pastel-shaded and supposedly heterosexual *Normal Love* (1963–   ).

Expanded Cinema

The third avant-garde continues, but a fourth has begun. It is not certain what its ultimate characteristics will be.

Currently it takes the form of film as environment, film as part of inter-media, film examined as a phenomenon of time and of light. It is sometimes called "expanded cinema."

In expanded cinema the mechanisms of cinema are used in new ways, as in the multiple projections of Stan Van-DerBeek's *Feedback # 1* (1965). Or there is an effect analogous to that of film, as in the environmental light shows that are spreading across the country, or as in Ken Jacobs's live shadow plays that reproduce the look of film. Expanded cinema is sometimes also deflated cinema, cinema from which everything but the bare essentials has been removed. Such is the case with the new stroboscopic style films that have no images, but only light and dark frames alternating in various patterns, as in Tony Conrad's *The Flicker* (1966), or as in Victor Gruen's *Archangel* (1966) and Paul J. Sharits's *Ray Gun Virus* (1966), which alternate solid color frames.

Into the Past/Into the Future

As cinema expands, as it begins to take in light shows and shadow plays, its history begins to include prefilmic techniques. These techniques go back to the shadow plays of Asia, to the possible use of light manipulation by priesthoods in ancient Greece, and perhaps to the time when prehistoric man played with his own shadow, when he first developed aesthetic reactions to light itself.

With expanded cinema there continues a progression towards complexity in film. The materials used in cinema are rapidly multiplying, and now include such things as videotape and computers. As the materials increase, the range increases. With the addition of new light media, such as television, the forms of cinema multiply. Film is only a form of cinema, and perhaps it will not be the dominant form for long. As more efficient and sensitive means of controlling light are developed, film itself may become extinct.

There has been a progression toward complexity. And there has been a progression toward simplicity. One may spend much to make a film. One may spend little. Jean Cocteau is supposed to have said that film will not become an art until its materials are no more costly than pencil and paper. That point is steadily approaching. As it approaches, freedom increases, and the personal art film becomes more vital.

In 1896 there was one personal film artist, Georges Méliès. There were perhaps fifty personal film artists during the first film avant-garde, and perhaps two hundred in America's second film avant-garde.

Now the number is incalculable.

This photograph of Kenneth Anger was taken by Chester Kessler, who ran the camera for *Fireworks* (although this photo was taken ten years later).

THREE: A Gallery of Film-Makers

Kenneth Anger
Born 1932, Santa Monica, California
Lives San Francisco, California

Kenneth Anger is called a film-maker, but calls himself a
magician. Film is his way of working magic, and he means
his films to be, quite literally, magical invocations. Sergei
Eisenstein is the inspiration behind his montage-oriented
technique. As for the magic, he pays homage to the late
English occultist Aleister Crowley (1875–1947).

Anger grew up in Hollywood, appearing in several movies
as a baby, and started making his own when he was nine. His
early works were *Who Has Been Rocking My Dream Boat?*
(1941), the hand-tinted *Tinsel Tree* (1941–42), a science-
fiction film with miniatures called *Prisoner of Mars* (1942),
a psychodrama about incest called *The Nest* (1943), another
psychodrama, *Escape Episode* (1944, re-edited, sound added
1946), which was his first film to be exhibited, and *Drastic
Demise* (1945) showing "sexually turned-on Hollywood
crowds on V-J Day." Ritual and magic were ingredients
even in these very early films.

Fireworks (1947) was made in Anger's home on three
nights when his parents were away. The film stock was
courtesy of the U.S. Navy, and the one backdrop had been
whisked away from the Columbia Studios backlot. Anger
plays an adolescent who dreams that he is beaten up and
eviscerated by a group of sailors. The name of the work
comes from the climactic scene where a sailor's penis becomes a shooting roman candle.

Anger's next five projects met with catastrophes. The planned feature on Hollywood of the twenties, *Puce Women,* survives only as *Puce Moment* (1948), a fragment in which a star chooses a gown and goes out "armored in jewels and wolfhounds," a ritual of assuming identity. *The Love That Whirls* (1949) was sabotaged by Kodak Laboratories, which confiscated color footage that showed a (faked) nude Aztec human sacrifice. Then he began in Paris, in 35mm, *La Lune des Lapins,* but lost the use of his sound stage, complete with the ornate set of a tinseled forest. *Maldoror* (1951–52), based on Lautréamont's poem of demon-maddened adolescence, was likewise unfinished, and a planned color film of Cocteau's *Le Jeune Homme et la Mort* (1953) subsists only in a black-and-white version, unshowable because of copyright restrictions.

He then made *Eaux d'Artifice* (1953) in the Villa D'Este Gardens of Tivoli in Italy. This film is described as "Hide and Seek in a night-time labyrinth of cascades, balustrades, grottoes, and leaping fountains, until the searching figure and the fountain become one," another rite of finding identity. The film is a beautiful fugue of water and light, cut to *The Four Seasons* of Vivaldi, shot in black and white, but printed on color stock through a blue filter and then hand tinted. The searching figure, gowned as a baroque court-lady, was actually a midget from a circus, chosen to make the scale of the gardens loom more spaciously. The moonlit nightscape was actually shot during afternoons.

Returning to Los Angeles, Anger made *Inauguration of the Pleasure Dome* (1954, recut 1966), a lavishly costumed magic masquerade party inspired by the neopagan rituals of Aleister Crowley. The various characters are from classical mythology, and as the celebration becomes an orgy, they become "high" on an LSD-like witches' brew and go through costume/make-up/personality changes, while the film itself enters a hallucinated crescendo of editing and superimposition. Three versions of *Inauguration* were prepared. The first "state" is a standard single-screen film. The second, shown in 1958 at the Brussels Experimental Film Festival, has a main screen flanked by "wings" (two smaller screens used for counterpoint) and uses three synchronized projectors. The third, edited in London in 1966, is the final "psychedelic" version and is calculated by the film-maker to be experienced under the effect of LSD. It has up to quintuple-imposition and uses added footage of the naked souls in Hell from *Dante's Inferno*, an early thirties Hollywood spectacle.

In 1955 the film-maker went to Cefalù, Sicily, to restore erotic frescoes painted by Aleister Crowley in his abandoned occult headquarters. Anger made a documentary for British television of the ruined temple and paintings, *Thelema Abbey* (1955), before the hostility of the superstitious peasants forced him to leave. His next project was *Histoire d'O* (1959–61), based on a modern French classic on sexual sadism. Although almost completed, that film remains hidden in France, because Anger is afraid that it would be seized if shown or exported.

Anger returned to the United States in 1962. According to astrology, 1962 was the end of the 2000-year-long Piscean Age and the beginning of the Aquarian Age, which occultists interpret as being the end of a period of Christian domination and the beginning of a period of Pagan domination. Anger made *Scorpio Rising* (1962–64), filmed in Brooklyn, editing completed in San Francisco, to invoke the breaking away from and purging of the old "sin-sickened" age by violence, destruction, and death, leading to resurrection in the new age. He saw pop songs, drug use, motorcycle cultists, the teen-age fad of Nazi symbols, and so on, as strong manifestations of fomenting demonic forces. The "hero," Scorpio, is intercut with shots of Hitler, James Dean, Marlon Brando (shown on a TV set in *The Wild One*), and Jesus Christ shown in scenes from a religious movie). A rough homosexual Halloween party of the cyclists is blended with footage of Christ meeting with his disciples, a cycle race with Jesus on the donkey entering Jerusalem. There is much detailed buckling of leather, roaring of motorcycles, flashing of red tail-lights, combined with glimpses of comic strip characters that reflect the mood of self-mocking self-destruction. The sound track is made up of pop songs. *Scorpio Rising* is a portrait of violence, an exercise in black humor, a document of motorcycle cultists, and one spectacular death wish—"a hymn to Thanatos."

Scorpio was re-cut and a film called *KKK*, for *Kustom Kar*

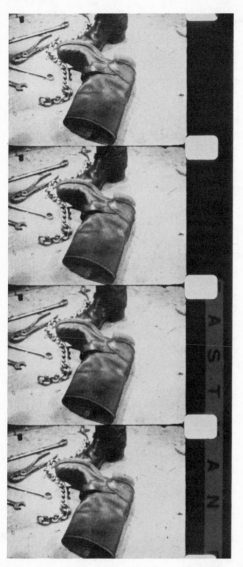

The early shots of *Scorpio Rising* threaten violence.

The threatened violence of *Scorpio* culminates in the death
of the cyclist at the end of the film.

Kommandos (1964–   ), was started when Anger received
a Ford Grant. He then went to London to prepare the LSD
version of *Inauguration* and to make *Anger Aquarian
Arcanum* (1965), a short sequence of magic symbols for the
prelude to his *Anger Magick Lantern Cycle*, which is a
compilation of his best work.

Currently he is in San Francisco working on *Lucifer Rising*
(1966–   ), a color feature about the "holy" war between
the two ages, Piscean and Aquarian, as represented by the
conflict between the "teeny boppers" and the adults. A
planned scene, for example, is of teen-agers kneeling along
the San Andreas Fault in California, praying for a liberating
earthquake. Anger calls it "my religious film."

In person Anger displays none of the violence that charac-
terizes his films. He surrounds himself, however, with magic
paraphernalia, as well as collections of books, posters, comic
strips, and pop objects that evoke violence. When not filming,
he usually screens and studies films in the European
cinémathèques.

Bruce Baillie

Born 1931, Aberdeen, South Dakota
Lives Berkeley, California

What forms the films of Bruce Baillie is his compassion and
concern for how people (and how nature) can exist in
today's environment. What provides the effectiveness of his
films is Baillie's ability to combine disparate images, simple
people and super weapons, harvests and circuses, whistling
highways and quiet sunrises, to make strong visual statements.

Until he was twenty-nine, Baillie had done little except
"wander around, draw and paint, make model airplanes, and
live in YMCAs." He served in the Korean War and took a
degree in art at the University of Minnesota in 1955. He
took several film courses at Minnesota and four years later,
in September of 1959, entered the London School of Film
Technique.

Four months later he headed for southern Spain to clear
his lungs of London air. He considered all the things he
hadn't done, and headed for San Francisco to make films.
He worked without pay for six months for a commercial

film-maker while he started his own first work, *On Sundays* (1960–61). The main character is a pretty Chinese-American named Miss Wong, and the half-documentary, half-dramatic plot concerns her discovery of, romance with, and desertion by an aging wino in San Francisco's Tenderloin.

Finding there was no organization among the Bay Area film-makers, Baillie started Canyon Cinema, an informal group that put on free public showings, and later put out *Canyon Cinema News*. A small but interested audience was built up in Berkeley as Baillie and others began to make short, localized films, which were called "news" films, to show to this specific audience.

His first "news" was *Mr. Hayashi* (1961), about an impoverished Japanese laborer whom he had seen wandering around Berkeley. Baillie began wandering with him, filming in the hills above the city, working in the light when the sun was beginning to burn through the fog. Later he added a simple sound track of Mr. Hayashi telling about his life and of Japanese samisen music. This was shown originally with *The Sculpture of David Lynn* (1961).

Next came *The Gymnasts* (1961), a mood piece with Baillie's first strong editing. *Friend Fleeing* (1961) was another short news and was followed by *Have You Thought of Talking to the Director?* (1962), a work involving both staged and documentary footage. The *Director* film was "about how society is always screwing up the good guys." *News # 3* (1962) and *Everyman* (1962) were both short assemblages showing Bay Area demonstrations. *A Hurrah for Soldiers* (1962–63) was a passion play in which an innocent is caught in the violent clash between cultures that have and those that have not. It was his first color film and was shot against low winter light to produce an achromatic effect. This was followed by another color work, *To Parsifal* (1963), which showed the sea and the Sierra Nevada Mountains.

He then made *Mass* (1963–64), a film dedicated to the Dakota Sioux but involving all contemporary life, showing an alien, "canned" environment. Baillie shot footage off television and movie screens, shot through fog filters, overexposed on purpose, and did everything to "keep things very diffuse." Certain sequences, involving a man slowly dying on a street and a motorcycle escorted hearse, were staged. All

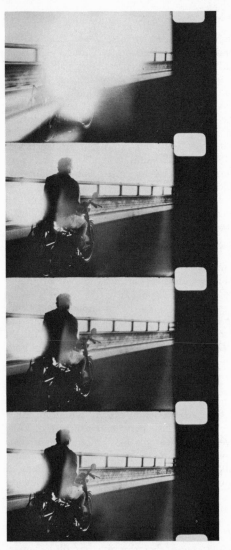

The motorcyclist in Baillie's *Mass* speeds compassion toward
an Indian dying on a city street.

footage was edited into definite segments corresponding to the form of the Catholic Mass.

Baillie then spent fifteen months making *Quixote* (1964–65), which at its simplest level is a visual trip across the United States. Actually it is a trip through the contemporary environment. The content is social, political, literary, personal, and aesthetic, with photography of laborers, movie serial heroes, karate blows, small-town basketball games, buffalo, and footage of the Viet Cong superimposed over New York City. It features at least one technical innovation, the use of superimpositional "wipes," achieved by applying opaque mylar tape to the A, B, and C rolls of simultaneous material.

Yellow Horse (1965–66) shows summer motorcycle events. *Tung* (1966), short and intense, works with continually moving macrophotography of natural objects passing in one direction while a girl in slow-motion negative passes in the other. Words of a poem appear like subtitles at the bottom of the screen. *Yellow Horse* and *Tung* are both breakaway films for Baillie as he leaves social and political content films behind, intending to involve himself more in the study of form. He is also trying to get away from the photograph, "as opposed to the living-moving frame." In *Castro Street* (1966), for example, he works with a malleable matte (a "matte" being a device used to block off an area of the lens of a motion-picture camera, usually used for trick effects), in the form of black gloves, so that irregular portions of the screen remain unexposed for later combination with other materials. Other films in this new direction are *Still Life* (1966), and *All My Life* (1966).

He made a *Newsreel* (1966) of the Port Chicago Napalm Vigil. This film is mostly *cinéma vérité* reporting of confrontations between the peace workers of the vigil and the men who make and carry the napalm bombs. He has also made a number of films for organizations, including schools, and most recently *Termination* (1966) for "the Indian people of Laytonville Rancheri." A 16mm sound-synch feature is presently in the works.

Baillie is a meditative person who works with a religious respect for his subjects and his materials. He photographs "what asks to be taken," and exposes by "what the particular film stock and form asks." During recent years he has supported himself with unemployment checks, ship-loading work, and now a Rockefeller grant. He is the unofficial anchorman of the West Coast underground.

Jordan Belson
Born 1926, Chicago, Illinois
Lives San Francisco, California

Jordan Belson is an almost legendary film-maker who has withheld the bulk of his films from exhibition. His beginning works were animated scroll paintings, and his latest resemble the Lumia compositions of Wilfred, but surpass them considerably in control, content, and intensity.

Belson became excited by the abstract works of Fischinger, Richter, and the Whitney brothers, which he saw at the 1947 Art in Cinema Series. Previously he had studied art at the California School of Fine Arts and had taken a B.A. from the University of California in 1946. His first films, *Transmutation* (1947) and *Improvisations # 1* (1948), have now been destroyed. Stopping to paint for four years, he continued with *Mambo* (1952), *Caravan* (1952), *Mandala* (1952–53), and *Bop Scotch* (1952–53), an experiment with animation of live objects.

He did film and light shows for the *Vortex Concerts* held in planetariums in San Francisco and Belgium, serving as Visual Director of the Audio-Visual Research Foundation from 1957 to 1959. In this time he produced *Flight* (1958), *Raga* (1959), and *Seance* (1959).

Since 1960 he has worked on six films. All these later films have been made with techniques of light manipulation and continuous (as opposed to stop-motion) photography. *Allures* (1961) is a "mathematically precise" film on the theme of cosmogenesis. Leftover footage from *Allures* went into the never completed *Illusions* (1962). *Re-Entry* (1964) deals with the subject of rebirth or re-entry into life. It is perhaps Belson's masterpiece. *Phenomena* (1965) is a dazzling display of visual phenomena. His newest works are *Samadhi* (1966–67) and an additional film not yet titled.

Belson thinks of his works as films "not to be seen, but to be experienced . . . not as creations, but as recognitions." In form they are to some extent the result of his studies of

Jordan Belson's *Allures* was the start of a new period for the film-maker, one in which he began to compose his own sound tracks.

Eastern mysticism, and in color and images possibly the result of psychedelic experiences.

Belson is a perfectionist and a recluse. He does not allow his films to be shown because he would be unable to control the environment of their projection or the quality of their audience.

Stan Brakhage
Born 1933, Kansas City, Missouri
Lives Rollinsville, Colorado

The films of Stan Brakhage present a rippling reality in which the photographic raw material of the film-maker's actual life is repeatedly transformed and reseen in a continual turbulence of movement, of color, of light. They are of such intense complexity that on one viewing they tend to be bewildering arrays of beautiful effects. To many poets and film-makers, however, the work of Brakhage has been, with its new ideas of vision, a mother lode of expanded techniques and fresh approaches.

Brakhage is involved with the idea of the camera, "ingathering light," being analagous to the eye, and film being analagous to vision. His idea of vision, though, is not confined to what the eye sees when open. It envelops "closed eye vision" as well, which includes such things as the flashing abstract patterns the eye sees when shut, visual memories, imaginations, hallucinations, daydreams and night dreams. With distorting lenses, scratching, painting, superimpositions, editing, and other methods of manipulating light, he has tried to put this composite vision on film.

Historically Brakhage is the major transitional figure in the turning away of "experimental" film from literature and surrealist psychodrama and in its subsequent move toward the more purely personal and visual. His early works, up through *Flesh of Morning*, were apprenticeships to the postwar generation. But he broke away, and with *Anticipation of the Night*, an attempt to show seeing without preconception, he established his own dizzying style. Since then he has produced an enormous variety of work, ranging from the nearly documentary *Window Water Baby Moving* birth film to the abstract *Pasht*, and from the hyperintricate *Dog Star Man* epic to the sweet and simple 8mm *Songs*.

Brakhage was adopted out of Kansas City, Missouri, when he was two weeks old. The marriage of the parents who adopted him was unstable, and his early years were spent in a number of midwest towns before he ended up in Denver. His mother used theatres as a convenient baby sitter, so Brakhage, aged seven, sometimes saw four movies a day. He left Denver to go to Dartmouth but had a nervous breakdown in his first semester there.

From then on he received most of his education from poets, painters, and film-makers. After making with Denver friends a simple boy-girl narrative called *Interim* (1953), he went to San Francisco to take a semester course in cinematography at the Institute of Fine Arts there. On a trip back to Denver, he made *Unglassed Windows Cast a Terrible Reflection* (1953), an expressionistic narrative. Much of his time in San Francisco was spent living in the basement of poet Robert Duncan and artist Jess Collins.

The real roots of Brakhage's style, the bobbing hand-held camera movement, the transformation of object and mood by distortion and rapid cutting, the titles scratched directly on film ("setting the basic cinematic pace of twenty-four frames per second at start") show up in *Desistfilm* (1954). This Denver-made account of a teen-age party is slightly naive but has a rollicking vitality.

Back in San Francisco, Brakhage made a less than successful slapstick comedy, *The Extraordinary Child* (1954), and then made *In Between* (1955), a portrait of Jess Collins edited to music by John Cage. It is a nightmare film in the second film avant-garde tradition, as is *The Way to the Shadow Garden* (1955), in which the hero blinds himself and everything is suddenly seen in eerie negative.

While still editing his last two films, he came to New York, where he got to know Willard Maas and Marie Menken, stayed with Maya Deren, and worked on films with Joseph Cornell. *Reflections on Black* (1955), made at that time, is about the imaginations of an "archetypical blindman." As he comes up stairs, oscillating scratches appear in place of his eyes, and in the apartments he passes nightmarish events occur between couples.

Joseph Cornell asked Brakhage to make him a film memento of the Third Avenue El before it was torn down. With Cornell's advice Brakhage made *The Wonder Ring*

(1955). This exquisitely photographed film was the beginning of a radical change for the film-maker in his interest in not telling, but seeing. He also did the photography on Cornell's *Towerhouse*, now called *June*.

Brakhage went to Denver and made a rarely seen film poem, *Zone Moment* (1956). Then he went to Los Angeles to work at Raymond Rohauer's theatre in exchange for room and board and screening rights to Rohauer's collection. He shot *Flesh of Morning* (1956–57), an intense, introspective, and totally controlled work about masturbation, and the striking *Nightcats* (1956), in which cats make abstract patterns as they move under floodlights in the night.

Following this came *Loving* (1957–58), an impressionistic portrait made in Denver of a couple entwined on the ground. As the camera swoops ecstatically around them, bursting shots of greenery are edited in. *Daybreak* and *Whiteye* (1957) are two exercises shown straight as they were photographed, with all editing being done in the camera. *Daybreak* is a jumpy portrait of a girl getting up at dawn and walking on New York's West Side. *Whiteye* is an exploration of a snowy Vermont landscape seen through a window, with rhythmic repetition of camera pans.

Anticipation of the Night (1958) shows a turning point in Brakhage's style. He tried to create, by complete fragmentation of the normal visual world, a new vision. There was a new fascination with light and increased reliance on editing. The resulting film caused a minor storm. Even experimental audiences would not look at it, and Cinema 16 refused to distribute it, helping to precipitate the founding of the Filmmakers' Cooperative. (Cinema 16 later distributed the film because of its historical role.)

During *Anticipation* Brakhage married, and his next film was *Wedlock House: An Intercourse* (1959). It showed in shadowy lighting an argument between his wife Jane and him, and was intercut with negative footage of them making love. This was followed by *Window Water Baby Moving* (1959), the powerfully graphic film of the birth of their first child. It shows Jane, pregnant, taking a bath, the birth of the child, and Brakhage's joyful face (photographed by Jane minutes after the birth).

Photographed before the birth film but edited afterwards were *Cat's Cradle* (1958–59) and *The Dead* (1958–60),

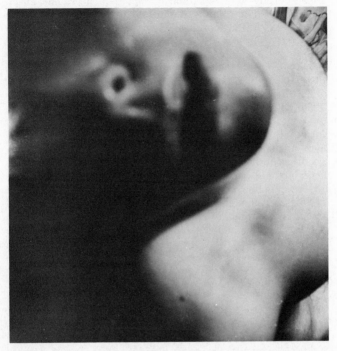

Masturbation was the subject of Brakhage's *Flesh of Morning*, one of his last "nightmare" style films. (*Collection* Film Culture)

both uncommonly beautiful. *Cat's Cradle* features single-frame cutting with repetition of shot sequences. *The Dead,* photographed in Europe during a trip to the experimental film festival in Belgium, is filled with somber rocking positive and negative shots of grey tombstones while superimposed in bright reds and blues the Seine dollies by. *Sirius Remembered* (1959) is mainly repeated pans and swooping dollies of a pet dog lying dead in the woods.

The birth of their third child became *Thigh Line Lyre Triangular* (1961). By painting and scratching over the images, Brakhage tried to put down what he actually saw, including bursts of colored light and other patterns of closed-eye vision. *Films by Stan Brakhage* (1961), subtitled "an avant-garde home movie," shows the Brakhages making love superimposed over pictures of their children and Jane's face superimposed over a green plant. *Blue Moses* (1962), one of his rare later films with a prewritten script and a sound track, is a curious examination of the relationship between life in the flesh and life on the screen. *Silent Sound Sense Stars Subotnick & Sender* (1962) is a portrait of Morton Subotnick and Ramon Sender, founders of the San Francisco Tape Center. *Oh Life, Woe Story, The A-Test News!* (1963) is a collection of images photographed off a television screen. *Mothlight* (1963) is a *tour de force*, a film made without camera. It was accomplished by pasting between strips of mylar tape a line of moth wings and bits of plants that was then run through an optical printer. The result is a fluttering light collage that Brakhage likes to say is "what a moth might see from birth to death if black were white."

Dog Star Man (1959–64) is Brakhage's major opus to date. Technically and thematically it is one of the most intricate seventy-eight minutes of film ever made, and like Joyce's *Finnegans Wake* would take a full book for exposition. Basically there is one action: a woodsman, played by Brakhage, climbs a hill and chops down a tree. But the film spreads out and repeats parts of that action, of the landscape, of the universe, with telescopic footage of the sun, the moon, the stars, of his family, of a beating heart, lungs, and bloodstream, and even of microscopic cells. Most of the photography was done in 1959–60 and then edited and re-edited into five sections, *Prelude* and *Parts One* through *Four.*

Prelude (1961) is a rippling superimpositional previews-of-coming-attractions/summary of the key images of the work. *Part One* (1962) is a long montage of the woodsman climbing the hill. *Part Two* (1963) is again superimpositional work, plus an innovation, dropping bits of cut-out film into individual 16mm frames, making actual collages, or as P. Adams Sitney has put it, "cutting within the frame." *Part Three* (1963) uses triple-impositions. *Part Four* (1964) brings the work to an accelerating close with quadruple-imposition, plus the cutting within the frame. And when Brakhage had finished *Dog Star Man*, he spread out all the superimposition rolls, showed them separate and showed them combined, making the four-and-a-half-hour *Art of Vision* (1961–65).

At this point Brakhage's 16mm camera was stolen, and he could afford to buy only a used 8mm instrument. This is how he switched to 8mm, planning a series of simple *Songs* with emphasis not so much on editing as on grain texture, camera movement, and in-camera editing. Eventually, however, he developed ways to do most of the things on 8mm that he had done on 16mm. The *Songs* now number twenty-three. The majority are three minutes long, but *Song 15* (1965), a collection of portraits called *15 Song Traits*, and the antiwar *Song 23* (1966), called *23rd Psalm Branch*, are both much longer.

Brakhage has continued with 16mm work. *Two: Creely/McClure* (1965) is a portrait of two poet friends (and in reduced-to-8mm form is part of *15 Song Traits*). The McClure segment consists entirely of single frame shots. The abstract *Pasht* (1965) looks like rippling red light, features the most splices per second of all his work, and is actually the recording of light patterns on the fur of a cat giving birth. *Three Films* (1965) includes *Blue White*, a birth film; *Blood's Tone*, showing a child nursing; and *Vein*, about a child masturbating. *Fire of Waters* (1965) is more ambitious. It is a sound film with thunder in the distance as day and night come and go in a controlled landscape of light. *Black Vision* (1965) is comparable to *Whiteye*, a careful explanation of a landscape, only with the more advanced techniques of distorting lenses, film painting and scratching, as well as the camera movement.

Presently Brakhage is finishing *Scenes from Under Childhood* (1966–   ). He is interested, because of the purity of

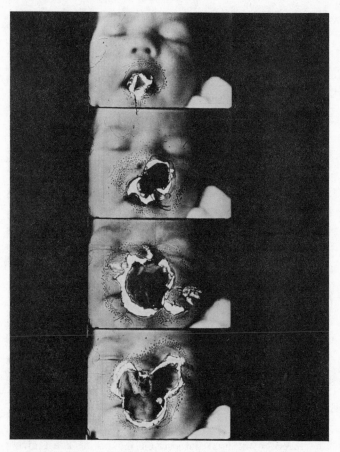

A crying baby comes out of the mouth of a crying baby in *Part Two* of Brakhage's *Dog Star Man*.

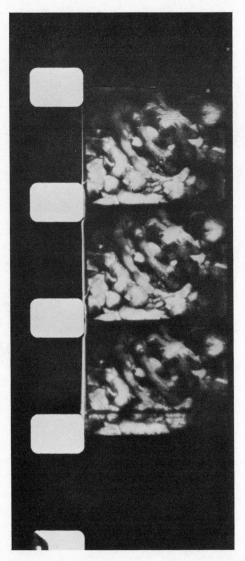

This shot of bodies in a concentration camp is from *23rd Psalm Branch*, Brakhage's longest 8mm work.

Brakhage is shown with his wife Jane, who herself photographs some of the scenes in his films. (*Collection* Film Culture)

the light, in making a painted film for laser projector (if somebody will invent a laser projector).

He is probably the most influenced and influencing of present-day film-makers. He exchanges films and letters with people in America and abroad, as well as giving lectures around the country. A volume of his writings, *Metaphors on Vision*, has been published by *Film Culture*.

Until 1964 Brakhage did occasional commercial film jobs. Now he concentrates on his own work and lives with his family in a ghost town nine thousand feet high in the Colorado mountains.

Robert Branaman
Born 1933, Wichita, Kansas
Lives Big Sur, California

Bob Branaman is a painter who makes films with the eye of an artist and the informality of a home movie maker. The subject matter of these films is his life, the places and people he knows. But their content is the dynamic throbbing and flow of light and space produced by his continual use of multiple-imposition and extremely rapid cutting, almost always improvised in the camera while shooting.

Branaman's introduction to film was in Wichita, in 1958, where he shot 8mm color rolls. Moving to San Francisco in 1959, he worked with Bruce Conner on several film projects. He made a three-roll *Wichita Film* (1960), now lost, and shot "a mess of rolls" in San Francisco. These included *The Filmore Bus* (1961), which was about the things you could see from the windows of a bus that went past his house. He continued shooting rolls after moving to Big Sur in 1962.

In 1964 he started thinking in terms of longer films, and began shooting, in 8mm and 16mm, a *Big Sur Movie* (1964–   ) that has never been finished. Out of this project came *Night Lights & Day Hi's* (1964–65), in 16mm, with sections of film scratching and others where psychedelic effects have been painted with analine dyes over moving landscapes. Also from that Big Sur project came *Gorda Adorg* (1964–65) in 8mm.

Branaman shot in 16mm *Goldmouth* (1965) around the poet Lawrence Ferlinghetti, doing his first extensive editing outside the camera. He intercut color, black-and-white, and

The face of Robert Branaman is superimposed over a self-portrait, creating in some degree the effect of his films. (*Horst Mayer*)

negative footage, scratched and painted over film, and even dropped little bits of other films within individual frames to make actual film collages. He also made a short 8mm work called *Ginsberg* (1966), which was shot in the company of poet Allen Ginsberg.

Branaman rarely makes prints of his films. Usually he shows originals until they are lost or exist no more. He lives on a hill overlooking the Pacific Ocean. His next film will star Michael McClure in *San Francisco Poets Nacked on Horse Back* to be shot at Big Sur.

Robert Breer
Born 1926, Detroit, Michigan
Lives Palisades, New York

Robert Breer produces animated films and time paintings with wit, eccentricity, and a curiously searching eye. The thing that has always annoyed him about moving pictures is that they (the pictures) move. Thus as a painter approaching cinema, he has chosen to define one unit of cinema as the viewing of a painting for 1/24 of a second, and to define a motion picture as several of these units viewed in sequence. The idea of lifelike continuity does not exist in his definitions or in many of his movies.

Breer makes "collage" films in which vast numbers of disparate images are rushed, rapid-fire, past the viewer, causing a sort of visual orgasm. And he makes "line" films in which calligraphic forms are animated through odd evolutions at a fixed rate and with a whimsical grace. There is constant change and constant transformation in all of Breer's films, but rarely conventional continuity. The result is that the collage films, such as *Image by Images I*, and the line films, such as *Par Avion*, and the various hybrids in between all defy either anticipation or memory.

Breer graduated in painting from Stanford in 1949 and then went to live in Paris. He started making films to record and animate his painting ideas, using a camera borrowed from his inventor father and an animation stand made from a lobster crate. First came *Form Phases I* (1953), *II & III* (1953), and *IV* (1954), all collage oriented. Then he made an outright experiment, *Image by Images I* (1954), photographing 240 completely unrelated single-frame images, pro-

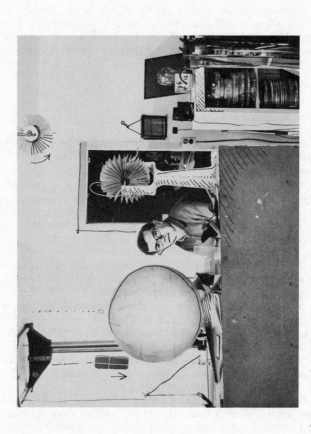

Robert Breer has retouched this photograph taken of him in his studio. (*Frances Breer*)

ducing a ten-second film that was probably the first to lack
any continuity whatsoever. This he projected as a loop and
was surprised to discover that his eye continually discovered
(imposed) new forms in the essentially formless material.

A *Miracle* (1954) came next, a fourteen-second satire on
Pope Pius, made with Pontus Hulten, and then more collage
films, *Image by Images II & III* (1955) and *IV* (1956), and
Motion Pictures (1956). His first line film was *Cats* (1956),
which was followed by pure collage exercises *Recreation I*
(1956–57) and *Recreation II* (1956–57).

Jamestown Baloos (1957) was a film that used all the
techniques Breer had developed so far and cleared the air
for the next, more accomplished works. These included
Par Avion (1957) and *A Man and His Dog Out for Air*
(1957), both line films, and *Eyewash* (1958–59), a collage
involving live photography and hand tinting of finished
prints.

Moving to Palisades, New York, in 1959, he continued
with *Homage to Jean Tinguely's Hommage to New York*
(1960), which subjectively detailed the construction and
reduction of a self-destroying machine event. He made
Inner and Outer Space (1960), another line work; *Blazes*
(1961), a collage of "100 basic images"; and his most (but
not very) conventional cartoon *Horse Over Tea Kettle*
(1962). With Claes Oldenburg's company of Happening performers, he shot a whacky live-action pop art venture called
Pat's Birthday (1962). Then came a line film, *Breathing*
(1963), and *Fist Fight* (1964), a film that again summed up
all his other techniques. His most recent film is *66* (1966).

Breer works inexpensively. His films, usually photographed
from flip cards, cost little more than home movies to make.
In addition to films, he makes variations of the old penny-
arcade Mutoscopes that show a cinematic sequence of images
or colors when the hand is cranked. Breer is friendly but
determined. He continues his love-hate relationship with
motion in his "floats," kinetic sculptures with a velocity so
refined that they seem not to move, but simply to change
location.

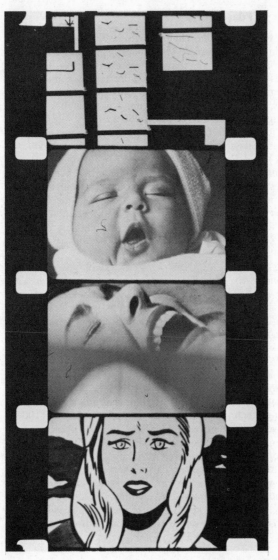

Every frame is an isolated image in Robert Breer's collage films, as in this strip from *Fist Fight*.

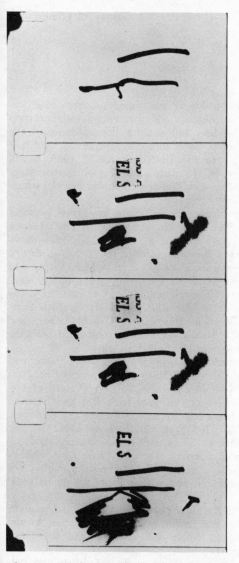

There is continuity from frame to frame in Breer's animated line work, as in these frames from *Breathing*.

Rudy Burckhardt
Born 1914, Switzerland
Lives New York, New York

Rudy Burckhardt makes simple, sometimes humorous documentaries and recently has collaborated on elaborate pop art fantasies. He has been influential in the underground, the influence being mainly one of unpretentiousness.

Burckhardt came to the United States in 1935, a still photographer by trade. He made a number of amateur slapstick comedies, ending with *Mounting Tension* (1950), which starred painter Larry Rivers.

For the next twelve years, he made low-keyed personal documentaries of New York life, starting with *The Automotive Story* (1953), intended as a spoof on television documentaries. Following this came *Under the Brooklyn Bridge* (1955), with a poetic sequence of naked children diving into the East River with Manhattan towering in the background. Filming what Joseph Cornell pointed out to him, he made *What Mozart Saw on Mulberry Street* (1956). *Eastside Summer* (1957), *Millions in Business as Usual* (1959), and *How Wide Is Sixth Avenue* (1962) were all filled with the everyday things one sees in Manhattan.

He lent his knowhow to Happening artist Red Grooms, and together they made *Shoot the Moon* (1962), a cross between Méliès's *Voyage dans la Lune* and MGM's *Wizard of Oz*. It used all the devices of the early trick film and featured Grooms's pop art papier-mâché sets, costumes, and direction. *Miracle on the BMT* (1963), starring Red and Mimi Grooms, was a partial return to Burckhardt's documentary style, although with some buffoonery. Then he made *Lurk* (1964–65), another pop art costume affair, starring Grooms as a Frankensteinlike monster, and with a script by dance critic Edwin Denby.

His latest film is the three-part *Good Morning, Hyacinth, and Junction*. The first shows midtown Manhattan in the morning; the second, female nude studies; and the third, a dance performance.

Burckhardt makes stills of art works for artists and galleries. He has taught classes in film and continues making his personal documentaries in New York City.

Red Grooms is seen resting between scenes in Rudy Burckhardt's *Lurk*.

Young ladies lay siege to Bruce Conner; presumably they are seeking a part in one of his films. (*Dennis Hopper*)

Bruce Conner

Born 1933, McPherson, Kansas
Lives San Francisco, California

Bruce Conner's *A Movie* and *Cosmic Ray* have been the most successful audience pleasers in the underground. Their popularity stems from their humorous juxtapositions, their spectacles of destruction, their use of "blue movie" material, all manipulated to achieve ironic effect. Bruce Conner's films please critic and voyeur alike.

Conner grew up in Wichita, Kansas, and received his B.F.A. from the University of Nebraska. He was living in San Francisco when he made *A Movie* (1958). Planned originally as a loop film to be part of one of his box sculpture constructions, it consists entirely of pirated stock footage of disasters and bizarre documentary material. It is grimly humorous, described as having "a kind of awful, deliberate grace," while *Cosmic Ray* (1961) is orgasmic in pace and content. *Cosmic Ray* uses some stock footage, too, but everything in the film, dancing girls, street lights, fireworks, goes by at a frenzied rate.

Conner moved to Brookline, Massachusetts in 1962 and eventually received a Ford grant. With this he made *Vivian* (1964), also photographed in fast motion, a picture about a girl dancing around Conner's work in an art gallery and eventually climbing into a glass case. The film is tightly edited to Conway Twitty's hit song, "Mona Lisa." Most of the Ford grant, though, was spent on *Report* (1964–65), which used footage and sound tracks on the Kennedy assassination. He started to do a complete documentary but had trouble with reproduction rights. *Report*, a very subjective film involving much repetition of scenes to rhythmic and ritual effect, was made instead. The work was re-edited before each printing so that there are at least eight different versions of *Report*.

His two latest works are *Looking for Mushrooms* (1960–66) and *Breakaway* (1966–67). *Looking for Mushrooms* has to do with peyote and was partially photographed by Robert Branaman. *Breakaway* is a portrait of a singer and dancer named Antonia Christina Basilotta. Conner sells an 8mm version of *Looking for Mushrooms*, plus three variations on

Cosmic Ray, #1 (in color), *#2* and *#3*. Each of these 8mm films was designed for cartridge projectors and has neither beginning nor end. (Cartridges operate on a "loop" principle.)

He has made considerably more than these works, but he prefers to show only his "public films" and not his "private films." Partly this is the result of a sense of supply and demand. Partly it is because once in Massachusetts while Conner was showing a film, "they unplugged the projector and took away the screen." He has made films that have been shown only once. He has made films that "I edited until they went away." He has made films that "I ran until they fell apart." He has made films that were for individuals, a work about Michael McClure given to McClure, and a work about George Herms given to Herms.

Now Conner is in San Francisco teaching at the Art Institute and planning a 35mm feature to be made with Shirley Clarke. He prefers playing the harmonica to speaking about his work but is the best self-publicist, save for Andy Warhol, of the film-makers. He frequently manufactures strange items, including a set of two buttons. The first reads, "I AM NOT BRUCE CONNER." The second reads, "I AM BRUCE CONNER."

Tony Conrad
Born 1940, Concord, New Hampshire
Lives New York, New York

Tony Conrad is the man who made *The Flicker*. *The Flicker* is a film made of pure black and pure white frames alternated in various patterns or frequencies. When projected, *The Flicker* causes a stroboscopic or "flicker" effect that can result in the eye's seeing nonexistent images and color patterns. Seeing *The Flicker* will cause one person in every fifteen thousand to have an epileptic seizure.

Conrad became aware of some of the effects of stroboscopic light in a class in the physiology of the nervous system at Harvard. Graduating from Harvard with a B.A. in mathematics in 1962, he went to New York to play the "drone violin" in La Monte Younge's avant-garde music group. He also began doing sound work for underground film-makers. He did the sound track for Jack Smith's *Flaming Creatures*,

WARNING.

The producer, distributor, & exhibitors waive all liability for physical or mental injury possibly caused by the motion picture "The Flicker."

Since this film may induce epileptic seizures or produce mild symptoms of shock treatment in certain persons, you are cautioned to remain in the theater only at your own risk. A physician should be in attendance.

This warning at the beginning of Conrad's first flicker film is followed by frames of solid dark and solid light.

brought in Angus MacLise to play the music for Ron Rice's *Chumlum*, and did a track for the yet unfinished *Normal Love* of Smith.

He discovered the more aesthetic effects of stroboscopic or intermittent light, or as he calls it, "flicker," when playing with a film projector that had variable speeds. He discovered that flicker begins at as low as four light flashes (frames) a second and that anything above forty flashes (frames) a second is indiscernible to the eye except as continuous light. He then made *The Flicker* (1965), a film that was nothing but flicker.

The Flicker is actually forty-seven different patterns of black and white frame combinations. It took two days to film the patterns and seven months to edit them. The resulting film starts with a high flicker rate of twenty-four flashes per second, causing little effect, but gradually lowers to a vigorously eye "massaging" rate of eighteen to four flashes per second. The flicker rate climbs toward the end of the film, returning the eye to a more peaceful environment.

Conrad has done a second flicker film, this one called *The Eye of Count Flickerstein* (1966).

Until receiving a Rockefeller grant, he worked as a computer programmer. He is married to Beverly Grant, an actress in many underground films.

Carmen D'Avino
Born 1918, Waterbury, Connecticut
Lives New York, New York

Carmen D'Avino's films of animated abstract paintings have, in a ten-year period, expanded into films of animated, painted, and pixilated environments. Following the early animated lines of Émile Cohl and Viking Eggeling, his highly colored designs flow with the rich detail and texture of a tapestry; and grow with organic vitality over a canvas (*Theme and Transition*), a window sill (*The Room*), and a player piano (*Pianissimo*).

D'Avino's playing with home movies while at the Art Students' League led to a World War Two job as a combat photographer that climaxed with his filming the Normandy Invasion and the Liberation of Paris. Studying painting in postwar France, he was stimulated by shorts, such as

Resnais's *Van Gogh*, which he saw in ciné-clubs, and after a 1948–49 painting trip to India, he enrolled in the École Technique de Photographie et Cinématographie in Paris. He made two never-completed documentaries, *Vernissage* (1950) about American painters in France, and *Finland* (1951) about forestry in that country, before returning to his native Connecticut in 1951.

Too exhausted by a night-shift factory job to both paint and make films, he compromised and produced his first abstract animated piece, *Patterns for a Sunday Afternoon* (1954). Excited by the possibilities of adding time and movement to his paintings, which, influenced by Indian art, already contained rhythmic and scroll elements, he made *Theme and Transition* (1956) and *The Big O* (1958). These were followed by *The Weavers* (1958), a work in which the lens was changed for every frame to achieve a fusing of colors and a sense of depth.

The Room (1958–59) was his first environmental film. During its ten-minute length (a year's laboring for the film-maker, who filmed each bit of design as it was laid down), a broken-down room becomes engulfed in an array of brilliant patterns that swarm over every surface. *A Trip* (1960) was the result of a mental block. Unable to work, D'Avino threw old exposed film into a bath tub, added color dyes and Cognac, scraped, stomped on, and sandpapered the footage. He cut what was left into two-foot lengths and finished by painting directly on the 16mm film.

He went back to the idea of animating within an environment with *Stone Sonata* (1962), where stones in a real forest magically move and are painted over. For *Pianissimo* (1963) he used the same technique on a player piano and a Venus de Milo, resulting in theatrical distribution and an Academy Award nomination.

Next he shot a story, based on a fable, in a real landscape and on 35mm film. This was *A Finnish Fable* (1964–65), financed by a Ford grant. While it was the most ambitious of his projects, involving stop-motion painting, animation of objects, and pixilation (that is, the animation of living things) of D'Avino himself, it was his least successful film in terms of audience response. However, it continued his direction, which seems to be toward a real world with reality completely moderated by the film-maker, his paints,

Carmen D'Avino meticulously applies a spot of paint to a dummy for his *Finnish Fable*.

and his camera. D'Avino's most recent film is the short short *Tarantella* (1966), on an Italian folk dance theme.

Besides his personal work, D'Avino makes films for corporations, including a two-minute animation piece on time for I.B.M. He works in his Manhattan apartment accompanied by wife, dog, and animation stand.

Ed Emshwiller
Born 1925, Lansing, Michigan
Lives Wantagh, Long Island, New York

The films of Ed Emshwiller, time paintings, dance works, poetic documentaries and statements, are all against the grain of today's experimental films. They are preconceived, precision shot, and tightly edited. They present a humming mechanistic vision, and seem to be the result of a man having made himself an extension of his camera.

Emshwiller likes and feels at home with machinery. He prefers to hand-hold his equipment while shooting, using a body disciplined like a dancer's as tripod, dolly, and boom. As cinematographer on *Hallelujah the Hills* he hand-held, for some scenes, a 135-pound sound camera. He often composes superimpositions in the camera and has the visual memory to do it.

At one time he was known simply as Emsh, and as such was one of the leading science-fiction illustrators in the world. Before that, during the Second World War, he was in the infantry. He graduated from the University of Michigan with a B. A. in Design in 1949, and studied painting at the École des Beaux Arts in Paris before working as an illustrator in the United States. He began making film "doodles" in 1952, and by 1956 was using the medium to keep records of painting and illustration development.

His first completed work was *Dance Chromatic* (1959), which had animated abstract paintings superimposed over a girl dancing. At the same time he made a time painting, *Transformations* (1959). *Life Lines* (1960) again involved live action and animated art work. Line drawings grew in anthropomorphic forms around artfully lit, often multiple-exposed studies of a nude model. *Variable Studies* (1960–   ), another time painting begun at this time, has yet to be finished.

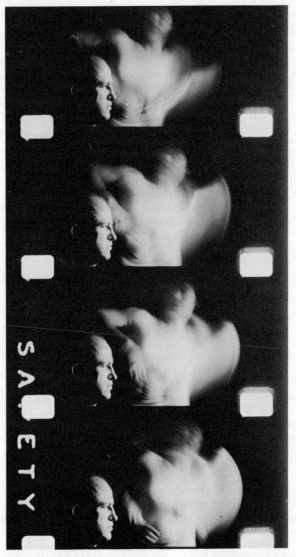

Emshwiller's *Thanatopsis*, like many others of this famous illustrator's films, has a ghostly, almost science-fiction quality.

As cinematographer on a low-budget 35mm feature, *Time of the Heathen* (1960–61), Emshwiller created dream and dance sequences in line with his personal work. This was followed by *Thanatopsis* (1960–62), perhaps his most technically remarkable work. Every movement in *Thanatopsis*, either by camera or dancer, was repeated again and again and photographed by single frame time exposure. The result is an eerie dynamic figure that waxes and wanes in alternately stable and vibrating environments. *Totem* (1962–63) is an impression of a dance work by the Alwin Nikolais Company and uses extensive editing to produce a shimmering, dramatic landscape of colors and bodies.

Scrambles (1960–63) is a grinding documentary about motorcycle contests. *George Dumpson's Place* (1961–63) is more poetic, being about an old Negro who collects junk. Hand-held dollying shots down green corridors, with piled-up artifacts, charge the film with a strange emotionalism.

Relativity (1963–66) is an experimental feature, made with the help of a Ford grant. It is a metaphorical work about man's place in the universe. Using ultrahigh-speed photography, pin-point lighting in black limbo, careful framing and superimposition, Emshwiller has achieved in *Relativity* complete visual control of time flow, gravity, and scale.

Emshwiller is generally recognized as being the best technician in the New American Cinema Group. He has been camera man for *The American Way* (1961), *Hallelujah the Hills* (1962), sections of *Film Magazine of the Arts* (1963), *The Streets of Greenwood* (1963), and *The Existentialist* (1964). He has made two films for the U.S.I.A. His live dance/film presentation, *Body Works* (1965), has the precision characteristic of his films.

Peter Emanuel Goldman
Born 1939, New York, New York
Lives New York, New York

Echoes of Silence is a long (eighty minutes) and brooding work that is more film novel than movie. Or it is a fresh kind of movie, made as books are written, with its maker slowly shaping and shooting what he saw or wanted to see. Cinematically it is unspectacular. Technically it is naive. But the film tells a story about a number of lives, most of them

Heir to Rossellini's neorealism, *Echoes of Silence* was made in the streets of New York and in the apartments of the actors.

unconnected except in their mutual isolation. And in the telling, in a series of fifteen simple and undramatic "chapters," it accumulates for the audience an overwhelming sense of human loneliness.

Peter Emanuel Goldman graduated from Brown University in 1960. He traveled around New York and Paris and eventually made an 8mm documentary about New York with his father's Kodak. That was his total film background when he began *Echoes of Silence* (1962–65).

He worked with a 16mm reflex, shooting mostly on out-of-date stock. The texture is grainy, the lighting dark. The figures of the characters, even during sexual contact, seem isolated. They move in an oppressive environment of Manhattan streets and Greenwich Village apartments. The action is understated but candid.

When the film was edited, each segment was preceded with a few printed lines of introduction or explanation. It is silent except for a music track added later. The film was made with documentary methods and materials, but the result transcends the simply documentary and makes it a one-of-a-kind work.

While finishing *Echoes*, Goldman began making other films. He produced two mood pieces about New York, *Pestilent City* (1965) and *Night Crawlers* (1964), the latter shot in slow-motion negative. He made a series of little comedies, like *Duncan Hines* (1964), which is a record of a black-tie picnic held on the floor of a subway train. *Reflections on a Mexican Vision* (1965–   ), a second narrative remains unfinished.

Goldman has begun professional film work now. He has worked as assistant cameraman and assistant editor on industrial films, and recently made a low, low budget 35mm sexploitation film, *The Sensualist* (1966). In terms of his personal films, he is presently of uncertain direction.

Ken Jacobs
Born 1933, New York, New York
Lives New York, New York

The work of Ken Jacobs has progressed from a cinema of manic despair to later, more visually controlled films. His early films, zany, grainy, and mostly starring Jack Smith,

Ken Jacobs is a violently opinionated person, and one of the secret *auteurs* of the underground. (*Peter Saladino*)

helped formulate an everything-goes style that declared, as Jacobs puts it, "What is art? It is not craft." Technically erratic, highly personal, and communicating an overwhelming sense of decay and moral deprivation, *Little Stabs at Happiness* and *Blonde Cobra* are greatly admired by film-makers, but not by audiences. And as neither of the above works, his best known, bear his name, and as it takes him from two to nine years to complete a film, his career has remained in archetypal underground obscurity.

Jacobs has spent most of his life around the environs of New York City. He grew up in a Jewish section of Brooklyn, and the songs and images of those days often show up in his films. His family life was "disastrous but typical, bequeathing me a social disgust and anger that I have cultivated, refined, momentualized, and am gagging on." It did not help that in a later time of supposed national wealth he was living off fish found at night on the streets of the Fulton Fish Market— and off of girl friends.

When seventeen he saw *Entr'acte* at the Museum of Modern Art and began writing screenplays. After serving in the most isolated possible Coast Guard station, a ship anchored off the coast of Alaska, he returned to New York and started the never finished *Orchard Street* (1956–). This was an unpretentious documentary about life on a Lower East Side market street, but nobody showed interest in it. And in fact Jacobs felt that "life was sort of kicking me out."

He was close to suicide, and he began to make films that communicated despair and that protested that despair with scenes of screaming *immediacy*. He used as his main non-actor a person who had tremendous on-screen presence, Jack Smith. His first film with Smith was *Saturday Afternoon Blood Sacrifice: TV Plug: Little Cobra Dance* (1957), which showed Smith dressed as a Spanish lady doing a frenetic dance, falling down, and being questioned by police, the last being an actual event incorporated into the film. *TV Plug* shows Jacobs showing his films on TV and was added in 1964.

His second Smith film was *Star Spangled to Death* (1957–), which still awaits final editing. *Star Spangled* was so torturously long that most of the audience walked out when versions were shown. Jacobs says he "wanted there to be always a question as to whether the film would last, would

Star Spangled to Death was photographed early in Ken Jacobs's career, but he was still editing it nine years later.

it die, would it at any moment fall off the projector?" In a different direction were the strange and tender short "poems" grouped together to make *Little Stabs at Happiness* (1958–61). The titles of the film give its maker as K. M. Rosenthal, a name perpetrated by Jacobs to "protect my obscurity."

In 1960 Bob Fleischner gave him some unedited footage Fleischner had shot of Jack Smith during nine afternoons in 1959. It showed Smith and others picking their way through a life environment of complete desolation. Jacobs edited the footage, added a sound track of Smith monologues and music from the thirties, occasionally running it over black leader. The result was the horrendous *Blonde Cobra* (1959–62). It is a work, says Jacobs, "about a life being crushed but winning by virtue of the audacity of its own self-statement." Jonas Mekas calls it "the masterpiece of Baudelairean cinema." Whatever it is, *Blonde Cobra* is unparalleled in its manic humor and hopelessness.

In the summer of 1961 Jacobs and Smith went to Provincetown to live on the beach. They opened a nightclub show called "The Human Wreckage Review," which the police closed. They had two rolls of film, and these became *The Death of P'Town* (1961), which showed frolics among dunes and cemeteries, with Jack Smith dressed as The Fairy Vampire. This was the last film Jacobs did with Smith. A subsequent work, *Baudelarian Capers* (1963–   ) was marred by defective equipment and film stock and is unfinished. And at this point, his 16mm camera was stolen, resulting in a switch to 8mm.

His first 8mm work was *The Winter Footage* (1964), a brooding contemplation of the world through a studio window with much use of calculated camera motion. Having been arrested as manager of a theatre showing *Flaming Creatures* in the spring of 1964, he became embroiled in the New York censorship controversy. Between court appearances he and his wife Flo lived in Southampton, Long Island. From that summer's footage of the greenery and of his wife came *We Stole Away* (1964). *Lisa and Joey in Connecticut: "You've Come Back!" "You're Still Here!"* (1965) was a portrait of Alfred Leslie and his family, intercut with sections of an old Mickey Mouse cartoon.

Jacobs started *The Sky Socialist* (1965–   ), which shows strongly controlled manipulation of objects and people in space. Part of the manipulation is done by using a zoom lens while panning, causing a compelling three-dimensional effect. *Naomi Is a Vision of Loveliness* (1965) is an 8mm roll of Naomi Levine, which Jacobs shows on a variable speed projector. Working with different lenses that can fragment, distort, or even cause the image to spill off of the screen, he produces a kind of visual meditation on this material.

Naomi is part of a new approach by Jacobs in which he treats cinema as controlled light. This approach is more apparent in his work with shadow plays. Here he achieves almost all the effects of film without camera or film. These shadow plays entail rear projection of live shadows and use the screen and the eye itself as camera and film. His main such piece is *Thirties Man: Chapter One of the Big Blackout of '65* (1965).

At times, when censorship has closed underground screenings, he has held shows of films in his loft, and he is developing private facilities for putting on shadow plays. He is also very interested in home movies as "folk art," and sometimes includes *Artie and Marty Rosenblatts' Baby Pictures*, a 1941 home movie, on his programs. He is "still busy discovering his star (and wife) Florencinio, and you wouldn't know he was sad to look at him."

Larry Jordan
Born 1934, Denver, Colorado
Lives San Anselmo, California

Larry Jordan is a determined explorer who has changed the direction of his film work a number of times. Starting with psychodramas, he has gone through very personal family-oriented films and on to highly accomplished animated collages, notably *Duo Concertantes*.

Jordan's introduction to films came through fellow high-school student Stan Brakhage, and during his one year at Harvard he was able to pick up beginning technique from the movie club there. Returning to Denver in 1953, he began a series of psychodramas that, at least at the start, were heavily influenced by Brakhage's early work. He made *Morning Game* (1954) and *The Child's Hand* (1954) before moving to San Francisco. There he continued with *The One*

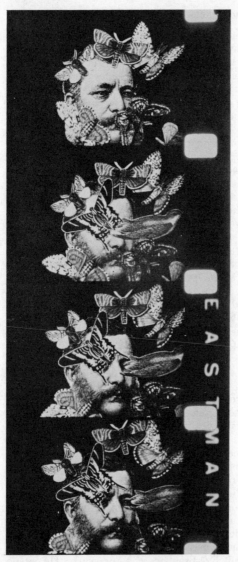

Old woodcuts and engravings achieve a magical fluidity of movement in Larry Jordan's *Duo Concertantes*.

Romantic Adventure of Edward (1955, recut 1957, 1965), *Man Is in Pain* (1955), *Trumpit* (1955–56), *3* (1955–56), and *Undertow* (1956).

While at sea in the Merchant Marine, he did a film poem, *Water Light* (1957). *Tryptych* (1958) is a visual journey that includes a peyote hunt film, and portraits of John Reed and the Wally Berman family. *Hymn in Praise of the Sun* (1960) is about the birth of his daughter.

Now living in San Francisco, he did a series of more private films that are usually not exhibited, including a series of portraits of friends. He did a scroll film, *Minerva Looks Out into the Zodiac* (1960), which appears to be a long pan around a series of motionless surrealistic landscapes. He also worked on *The Forty and One Nights, or, Jess's Didactic Nickelodeon* (1960–63) with Jess Collins, with collages flipped in Mutoscope style.

After moving to Larkspur, California, he did his first animated film, *The Monkey*, which was actually part of *The Movie Critic* (1961). And from leftover footage, he put together the feature-length *The Circus Savage* (1961), a work meant to be run as background or environmental cinema.

Moving to San Anselmo, he did *Jewelface* (1962–64), a portrait of George Herms, and began work on the collage series. Using rustic and nostalgic (almost necrophilic) materials juxtaposed surrealistically, as in the photo-collages of Max Ernst and Jess, he produced films animated with an eerie fluidity. The first was *Duo Concertantes* (1962–64), containing *Patricia Gives Birth to a Dream by the Doorway* and *The Centennial Exposition*. After that came *Dream Merchant* (1964), *Pink Swine* (1964), *Ein Traum de Liebenden* (1964) (translated *A Dream of Lovers*), and *Hamfat Asar* (1965).

Jordan is involved with the mystical and the supernatural. His latest project is a featurette ghost story, shot during the summer of 1965, with four people alternating as director. He has also spent time working on films with Joseph Cornell. He paints and recently has been making box sculptures in the style made famous by Cornell. He has printed privately two books with selections of stills from *Ivan the Terrible* and *Orphée*.

The missile base that looked so threateningly real in *Georg* was actually a set built by the girl who played the female lead. (*Collection* Film Quarterly)

Stanton Kaye
Born 1943, Los Angeles, California
Lives New York, New York

Stanton Kaye's *Georg* (1964) is a film that is strengthened by its lack of finish. It is presented as an hour-long home movie put together by a German immigrant to America. Georg compulsively and candidly records on film and tape the whole of his life, including the solitary burial at dawn of his wife and still-born child, and his own death, with the camera still running, as he makes a naive dynamite attack on a missile site.

Georg is a work of fiction, but the look and sound of its crude and intimate immediacy makes it seem overpoweringly real. The occasional sequences of overt artiness and technical facility in it usually go unnoticed. Some people believe the film to be an actuality.

Kaye grew up in Southern California. A sometime student at U.C.L.A.'s film school, he unsuccessfully sought help there to make *Georg* when he was eighteen. At the time he intended to play the lead himself and to actually kill himself in the last scene with the camera recording it. Two years later he was able to complete the film, but with an actor playing the part of Georg and with an acted death. This was Kaye's first film.

He does not show his second, a narrative done at the film school. It is titled *Greed* (1964) and has a vague connection with the Frank Norris novel of the same name. He has made *Brandy* (1966) about a girl friend, and is planning a remake of *Greed*. This will be called *Gold* and will again use the approximately Pirandellian and Brechtian approach of *Georg*.

Mike and George Kuchar
Born 1942, New York, New York
Live New York, New York

The Kuchar Brothers make Hollywood movies, or, facsimiles thereof. Teen-age and unknown, they began producing in the Bronx 8mm parodies of the movies they saw three and four times in a row in their neighborhood theatres.

Filled with gorgeous home movie color, overacted by a stock company of neighbors and friends, the Kuchar movies are filmed with an innate grasp of Hollywood movie artifice in matters of timing, camera angles, and plotting. Grotesquely violent and naive fantasies that star real people in real Bronx places, their works have been called folk art, pop art, and "pure Americana."

The Kuchar Brothers are twins. From ages eight to thirteen they spent all their spare time in movie theatres, developing in the process a keen appreciation for the forms and affectations of Hollywood. Mike liked the fantastic colors and pounding Max Steiner sound tracks of the Warner Brothers product, while George preferred the cheap black-and-white drama of Republic Pictures' detective movies.

When twelve they began to make fifty-foot 8mm slapstick costume pieces, such as *The Wet Destruction of the Atlantic Empire* (1954). They began to make longer movies with *Screwball* (1957) and *The Naked and the Nude* (1957). These early films were pretty much improvised, as was *Screwball*, which was planned as one long love scene. It got boring, however, so they had the hero go insane and choke the heroine to death.

By age sixteen the Kuchars were turning out works consistent with their Hollywood-in-the-Bronx aesthetic. For these pictures they discovered their own kind of stars, people "who were fat, but they wanted to be Marilyn Monroe." Together they made *The Slasher* (1958), *The Thief and the Stripper* (1959), *A Tub Named Desire* (1960), *I Was a Teen Age Rumpot* (1960), and *Pussy on a Hot Tin Roof* (1961). The later the film the more elaborate the plot. In *The Thief and the Stripper*, for example, a painter murders his wife because he wants to go with a stripper, while the stripper falls in love with a burglar, and everybody gets killed as it is revealed that the stripper is the sister of the murdered wife.

Gradually the Kuchar Brothers began to work separately. They worked on each other's films, but each film was definitely directed by one or the other. As their work has matured, each has developed a definite style. Mike likes color and visual spectacle. George likes steamy drama.

Mike made *Born of the Wind* (1961) and *The Pervert* (1963) before switching to 16mm. His first film in 16mm was *Sins of the Fleshapoids* (1964), which had a cast of

Mike Kuchar's films are often filled with the visually spectacular, as in this spider-web set from *The Secret of Wendel Samson* which symbolized hero Red Grooms's sexual entanglements.

Brother George Kuchar prefers the passion-filled plot; witness this shower scene from *Hold Me While I'm Naked* with Donna Kerness and Hope Morris.

over-ripe women and robots that were on their way to taking over the world. This was followed by *Green Desire* (1965), *The Secret of Wendel Samson* (1966), about a secret homosexual who is forced at gunpoint to make love to a woman, and *Madonna* (1967).

George's first independent film was *A Town Called Tempest* (1961), which featured a remarkably effective special-effects section of a tornado destroying a town. This was followed by *A Woman Distressed* (1962), *Lust for Ecstasy* (1963), *Anita Needs Me* (1963), and *The Lovers of Eternity* (1964). After switching to 16mm, he made *Corruption of the Damned* (1965), *Leisure* (1966), *Hold Me While I'm Naked* (1966), *Mosholu Holiday* (1967), which was made for Canadian Television, and *Eclipse of the Sun Virgin* (1967).

Unlike their tortured characters, the Kuchar Brothers are rather gregarious. Mike has worked in a photo retouching lab and George as a chart maker for NBC weather programs. Both now devote full time to making films, and are able to live on the income from their films.

George Landow
Born 1944, New Haven, Connecticut
Lives New York, New York

While most film-makers work within one tradition or another, George Landow is on his own. No one else makes films like Landow, possibly because, although he utilizes the materials and possibilities of film, what he makes are not exactly films. What he makes are curious visual explorations. They are explorations of a single moment of film, for example, by means of a loop. Or they are explorations of a single image made by packing one film frame with ten film frames.

Landow made two films in high school. One of them was called *Faulty Pronoun Reference, Comparison and Punctuation of the Participle Phrase*, which compared three commonly made grammatical mistakes with three persons who were making them. The later films are simpler than this, and are, in fact, based on simplicity of approach. They involve a static camera and one image, with variations of that image with regard to color, exposure, size, and framing.

His 8mm *Are Era* (1962) is simply flash frame close-ups

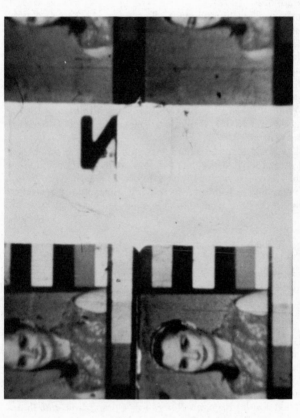

This is one frame from George Landow's Film in Which There Appear Sprocket Holes, Edge Lettering, Dirt Particles, Etc.

of a television commentator fluttering by at high speed. The 8mm *Richard Kraft at the Playboy Club* (1963) is the same thing, only with a real man's face superimposed over a television screen. Again the face flutters, jumps back and forth, and changes in exposure and framing, building a dynamic impression of the one image.

Continuing with Kraft's face, Landow made the 16mm *Fleming Faloon* (1963), which shows the same variations, only simultaneously. This was done by combining and filming on a screen a complexity of frames, achieving ten similar but separate frames in one. He then made the 8mm *Fleming Faloon Screening* (1963–64), which showed the film being shown in a room, and which contrasted the movie images with the interior of the room. "The people in the room are once removed from us. The person in the movie is two and three times removed."

Following this came *The Leopard Skin* (1964–65), which is a leopard skin filmed so that the spots flash on and off making "something happen optically." *Not a Case of Lateral Displacement* (1965) is a static 8mm consideration of a skin infection. *Adjacent Yes, but Simultaneous* (1965) is an 8mm film in which the right half of the film is happening in a different place from the left half, though both are happening at the same time.

Landow made a 16mm loop film called *This Film Will Be Interrupted After 11 Minutes by a Commercial* (1965), which was to be run 22 minutes with a Dutch Masters Cigar television commercial inserted in the middle. Made from a split 35mm Kodak test film that showed two and a half pictures of a model batting her eyelashes, with sprocket holes in the middle, it allows the audience to get a unique and continuous feeling of a single moment of film. It was shown this way only twice, and then was optically printed into a film called *Film in Which There Appear Sprocket Holes, Edge Lettering, Dirt Particles, Etc.* (1965–66). The title is accurate.

Landow studies art at the Pratt Institute. In addition to films, he makes constructions and other three-dimensional works.

Gregory Markopoulos, a personal film-maker of twenty-plus years, is seen preparing to do a take for his film *The Illiac Passion*. (*Jerry Hiler*)

Gregory Markopoulos
Born 1928, Toledo, Ohio
Lives New York, New York

Gregory Markopoulos has centered his films on themes of "male love," using as his point of departure Greek mythology and literature. His photography is marked by an extreme richness of composition and of color. His editing is notable for its intercutting of brief shots of present, past, and future, which results in a spreading of consciousness. Although he may have a series of events in mind, their fragmented presentation seems more the exploration of an emotion than the telling of a story. Increasingly, in *Twice a Man* and *The Illiac Passion*, he has made use of bursts of contrapuntal single-frame image clusters that go by at machine-gun speed and act in the films as *leitmotifs* do in music.

Markopoulos grew up in Toledo, Ohio. Greek was the language of the household, and he learned to speak it before he learned English. When he was twelve he began making short 8mm story films, including a version of Dickens's *A Christmas Carol*. In 1945 he entered the University of Southern California in Los Angeles. Though not seen much in classes, he stayed there two and a half years, using the money meant for his second year's tuition to make films.

Psyche (1947–48), based on an unfinished novelette by Pierre Loüys, was the first film of a trilogy on love between people of the same sex (Psyche is meant to be a lesbian), *Du Sang de la Volupté et de la Mort*. It was put together without viewer or splicer, but is quite visibly the beginning of Markopoulos's style. The framing is dramatic, the concern with color evident, and at the end there is a sequence in which all the major scenes of the film are rapidly recapitulated.

Lysis (1948), the second of the trilogy, inspired by Plato's dialogue on friendship, is a fragmented memoir, a series of strikingly framed shots, all unmoving, all the same length, of nostalgic objects and scenes. It is shown as it was photographed, with no editing. *Charmides* (1948), based on Plato's dialogue on temperance and photographed in a weekend at the University of Toledo, is the third and most conventional film of the trilogy.

Some less known works followed. One was *The Dead Ones* (1948), photographed on black-and-white 35mm film. One was *Xmas USA 1949*, which became *Jackdaw*, which became *Father's Day*, and finally ended as *Flowers of Asphalt* (1951).

His next film was *Swain* (1951), one of Markopoulos's tightest and most easily appreciated works. Inspired by Hawthorne's novelette *Fanshawe*, it shows the world of a mystic youth, played by the film-maker, in moodily dark colors. As the film progresses in rapid and rhythmic cuts, it builds a spell of desire and desperation unto insanity. After *Swain* he made *Eldora* (1952), a little seen piece on the sexual awakening of an adolescent girl.

In 1954 he went to Greece, where he decided to make *Serenity* (1955–60), based on a novel of Elia Venezis about the forced Greek migration of 1921. He secured wavering commercial support and attempted to photograph it in 1958, but was forced to end shooting before he had done all the necessary scenes. The next three years were spent trying to obtain the rushes to edit, then to retain possession of the film after editing. Two versions of *Serenity* were prepared, both with simultaneous four-language narration, both in the Markopoulos fashion of blended present, past, and future. (He did not manage to retain possession of his work.)

Twice a Man (1962–63), a feature, was inspired by the Hippolytus myth. A synopsis published in *Film Culture* states "construction of the film interweaves the thoughts and memories of Paul (the hero), his mother, and his mentor, so that no clear differentiation is made between memory and reality." The film includes a fragmented sound track to go with the images.

The most ambitious work of Markopoulos to date is *The Illiac Passion* (1964–66). It stars Andy Warhol, Clara Hoover, Jack Smith, and many other personalities. "Around each revolves a human situation. The sum total of the film is a sum total of the human passions," says Markopoulos. Deca-impositioning, single framing, and "three continuous and alternating streams of imagery" are used. While waiting for the expensive process of printing *The Illiac Passion*, he did a 35mm short, *The Death of Hemingway* (1965), based on a play by George Christopoulos. The negative was scratched to give the appearance of rain. Although the film-maker does not like the film, certain clusters of single-frame shots are impressive.

Recently Markopoulos did thirty film portraits, each three minutes long, of famous contemporaries and friends, including Jasper Johns, W. H. Auden, and collector Robert Scull. This has been released as *Galaxie* (1966). A series of grants has allowed him to complete several other films. One is a feature, *Himself as Herself* (1966), based on Balzac's novel *Seraphita* and shot in two and a half weeks. Another is a short, *Ming Green* (1966). He has begun work on *Eros, O Basileus* (1966–   ).

Markopoulos has publicly disassociated himself from the term "underground," not surprising considering he was making films fifteen years before the term came into use. He considers himself not consciously influenced by or related to any other film-maker. He is a classicist and a romantic. Recently he has been a Visiting Associate Professor at the Art Institute of Chicago in film.

Jonas Mekas
Born 1922, Semeniskiai, Lithuania
Lives New York, New York

When writing Jonas Mekas acts the role of the wild visionary, but his films tend toward the gentle and the documentary. While he did make the much discussed avant-garde feature *Guns of the Trees,* and his most often seen film is *The Brig,* a violent *cinéma-vérité* record of a violent stage production, most of Mekas's films are personal newsreels, records of people and events around the New York art scene. The most enthusiastic defender of other underground film-makers, he says of himself that he has "just worked around the edge of cinema."

Following a brief career as resistance newspaper publisher and concentration camp prisoner, Mekas began studying films during five years spent in displaced persons camps. He continued that study after coming to the United States in 1950. He began on his third day in this country to make films, and has been involved in numerous related activities ever since, often to the exclusion of film-making.

His first works were a documentary about Brooklyn called *Grand Street* (1953) and *Silent Journey* (1955), a narrative.

A prisoner goes berserk in Mekas's film of Kenneth Brown's play *The Brig*.

After much written support of independent features, he made the experimental *Guns of the Trees* (1960–61). It has a disjointed story, an elliptical form, and a message of protest. He considers it unfinished and may recut it in the future.

His next project was *The Secret Passions of Salvador Dali*. For two years Mekas filmed the artist whenever he was in New York. This footage is being edited into *100 Glimpses of Salvador Dali* (1961–   ). A Dali shooting session at a demonstration of moiré patterns by Professor Oster has been set apart as *Moires: Dali/Oster Newsreel* (1963).

Mekas was commissioned by *Show Magazine* to do a promotion film for certain products shot against art events. He was more interested in the events than the products, however, and the resulting film was destroyed by *Show*. Mekas was left with a work print. Suffering somewhat in photographic quality from its work print status, *Film Magazine of the Arts* (1963), shows events such as a Happening (with time-lapse photography), an art exhibit, and a dance concert.

After this came *The Brig* (1964), the film version of a Living Theater production of Kenneth Brown's play about military brutality. The production was so tightly rehearsed that Mekas treated it as a reality. Shot hand-held in a single evening, *The Brig* looked so grindingly real that the Venice Film Festival voted it the best documentary of 1964.

Mekas has also made *Award Presentation to Andy Warhol* (1964), which documents Warhol's receiving the Sixth Independent Film Award and does it in Warhol's style. His most recent films are *The Millbrook Report* (1966), on a raid on the Millbrook headquarters of Dr. Timothy Leary, *The Circus Notebook* (1966), and *Hare Krishna* (1966).

In addition to Mekas's formal pieces, there is his film diary, kept from 1950 to the present. It is now seven hours in unedited length. The 1963 section is being made into *A Fool's Haikus* (1963–   ).

Mekas assisted his brother Adolfas on *Hallelujah the Hills* (1963), and Adolfas did the sound editing on *The Brig*. Mekas has made bit appearances in a number of independent films, including his brother's *Double Barreled Detective Story*.

Marie Menken
Born 1910, New York, New York
Lives New York, New York

Marie Menken makes little films for a circle of friends. Yet her works deal so directly with the basics of film, with light and with motion, that they have gained a much wider audience. At once essays, exercises, explorations, and perhaps poems, her films vary widely in technique and subject matter. But whether they are a moving picture postcard (*Bagatelle for Willard Maas*) or a stylized biography (*Andy Warhol*), whether they use camera motion (*Visual Variations on Noguchi*) or object motion (*Go Go Go*), they have in common a lyric lightness and a love for jolting visual rhythms.

A carpenter's daughter with can-do skills, she quickly mastered Francis Lee's camera when he gave it to her in the form of a pawn ticket. She did the photography on husband Willard Maas's *Geography of the Body* (1943) and used that film to get a job as miniature and special effects expert on Signal Corps movies.

Her first personal film was *Visual Variations on Noguchi* (1945), in which photography and editing make the sculptures of Isamu Noguchi "move" through light. (Originally this footage was to be the backdrop for a John Cage–Merce Cunningham dance piece.) Twelve years went by, and then she continued with *Glimpse of the Garden* (1957), its title describing its contents. *Hurry! Hurry!* (1957) was made next and is a microscopic investigation of human sperm cells lashing around in search of an egg, double-exposed over flame and with a sound track of bombardment. And in the style of Francis Lee, she made *Dwightania* (1959), with materials animated over the work of painter Dwight Ripley.

Eye Music in Red Major (1961) was made with unmoving flashlights and a moving camera. *Arabesque for Kenneth Anger* (1961) is a tour through the Alhambra in Granada, a Moorish Palace, the camera catching the flare of the architecture and showing the things Anger was pointing out to Menken at the time. *Bagatelle for Willard Maas* (1961) is the same, but it is about Versailles, which like Menken's husband "is very precious. Also rather naughty and rather wicked." *Mood Mondrian* (1961–63) is a camera exploration of Mondrian's painting "Broadway Boogie Woogie." *Drips and Strips* (1961–65) is the objective recording of compositions made by dripping colored strips of paint down a surface.

Notebook (1962–63) is a film-maker's equivalent of a writer's journal. It is a collection of short pieces, some technical experiments, some lyric recordings. *Go Go Go* (1963) is a study of patterns of motion, being a look at New York speeded up. Included are striking time-lapse shots of Staten Island ferries moving over the harbor like skating steam-irons over a pond. *Wrestling* (1964), a time-lapse recording of television wrestling, is a remarkable commentary on what is real (for the camera keeps trying to pan with the action) and on how to frame (there is tension between the television framing and movie framing). *Andy Warhol* (1965) is a time-lapse portrait of Warhol, his crew, his art, and his "factory."

Menken has a number of unfinished works. *Faucet* (1960–) shows a dripping faucet, *Sidewalks* (1961–) speeded up pedestrians, *Zenscapes* (1962–) a Japanese rock garden, *Moonplay* (1962–) various animations, and *Lights* (1965–), lights at night. Other unfinished films are "parked" in *Notebook*.

In addition she has worked on all her husband's films (Willard Maas is again in production with an "epic and several shorts") and has acted in them and in others, including Lederberg's *Eargogh* and Warhol/Tavel's *Juanita Castro*. She has supported the activities of the family Gryphon Productions with twenty years at *Time Magazine*. She is also a den mother for many New York film-makers.

Robert Nelson
Born 1930, San Francisco, California
Lives San Francisco, California

New to film-making, Robert Nelson has already established a tendency toward the zany and humorously obscure. His *Oh Dem Watermelons*, an assault on conceptions about Negroes and movies, compares with René Clair's *Entr'acte*.

Nelson is a painter who graduated from San Francisco State College and studied at the San Francisco Art Institute and at Mills College. He eased into film-making with 16mm home movies, then joined others from the Bay Area interested

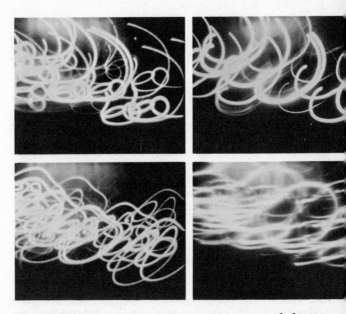

Marie Menken's moving camera turns stationary lights into kinetic patterns in this four-frame sequence from *Lights*.

This young lady, enjoying the pleasures of a good water-melon, is from Robert Nelson's *Oh Dem Watermelons*. (*Bill Menken*)

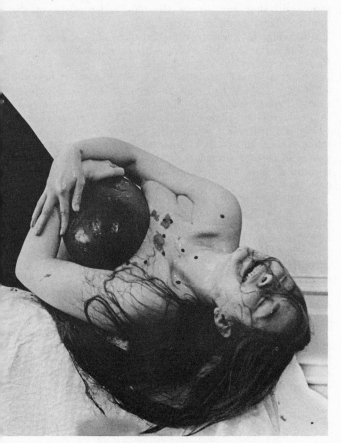

in film, including Ron Davis, the founder of the San Francisco Mime Troupe, and painter Bill Wiley. *Plastic Haircut* (1963), their first film, was "a series of absurd images," with various characters moving through abstract sets created by sculptor Robert Hudson and Wiley.

Oh Dem Watermelons (1965), made to be an interlude in the Mime Troupe's *A Minstrel Show*, was equipped with music by Steve Reich and featured actors from the show. The real stars, however, are fifteen watermelons that are, with satiric intent, mangled and spattered in gleefully edited sight gags that have made the film, independent of the minstrel show, an underground hit.

Following this Nelson worked on three films at once. One was *Thick Pucker* (1964–65), with candid footage of San Francisco edited to a sound montage by composer Steve Reich. One was *Confessions of a Black Mother Succuba* (1964–65), which had vast amounts of "soft core pornography" footage blended in uncongealed themes of violence, sex, and television commercials. *Oiley Pelosa the Pumph Man* (1964–65) features a weird central image of a man rocking intently back and forth in front of a target while an automatic device fires a revolver at his head. Also memorable are pastoral shots of two quite naked women swinging joyously on a rope.

Nelson then made another batch of films, finishing them again at about the same time. The longest of these is *The Great Blondino* (1966–67), about the man who pushed a wheelbarrow across a tightrope over Niagara Falls in 1859. The others are *Hot Leatherette* (1966–67); *Jimmy Witherspoon & Penny Bright* (1966–67), "movie loops ever tighter until the eye will rebel"; *The Off-Handed Jape* (1966–67), "a how to act absurdity"; *Super Spread* (1966–67), with a sound track by The Grateful Dead rock group; *Half Open and Lumpy* (1966–67), and *Awful Backlash* (1966–67).

Nelson has taught painting in San Quentin Prison, among other places, and now teaches film at the San Francisco Art Institute. His wife Guvnor has, with Bill Wiley's wife Dorothy, made a film called *Schmeerguntz* (1965), which satirizes the modern woman.

Ron Rice
Born 1935, New York, New York
Died 1964, Acapulco, Mexico

Ron Rice was one of the major talents of the New American Cinema, and, it is said, a character of primitive forcefulness. His films, while lacking in technical certainty, are packed with images that communicate a brute power. He made only a few films before his death. Each is a melange of humor, of discontinuous drama, and of spectacular visual beauty. The glue that holds them together is a wildly poetic vision and composition that frames perfectly a movement or a moment.

Rice did not finish high school. Initially he was very involved with bicycle racing and in 1958 bought an 8mm camera to film races. In the summer of 1959 he went to Provincetown and made a movie that was partly about a painter's exhibition and partly footage of a girl running nude through the sand dunes. That winter he headed West with 16mm equipment to photograph the Winter Olympics at Squaw Valley, California. What he shot was never developed, and he went on to San Francisco.

There he met Vernon Zimmerman, who helped him with *The Flower Thief* (1960), and Taylor Mead who starred in it. Existing in two versions, one of which is feature length, *The Flower Thief* shows Mead wandering through alternately wistful and humorous hi-jinks, a sort of "beat" saint.

Back in New York, Rice went to work on a film called *The Dancing Master* but became discouraged with it. He made *Senseless* (1962) next, shooting mostly in Mexico. *Senseless*, "filmed in super antirealism," made no sense to the mind, but it did to the eye. It is perhaps the most beautiful of his films, and is, as well, a sort of informal documentary of the life and diversions of the on-the-road hipster. In Rice's usual non-sequitur style, he included footage from *The Dancing Master*.

Rice began another film in New York, *The Queen of Sheba Meets the Atom Man* (1963–   ), with Taylor Mead. Over one hundred minutes of a projected three hours were shot and shown in rough cut at a benefit. The benefit yielded

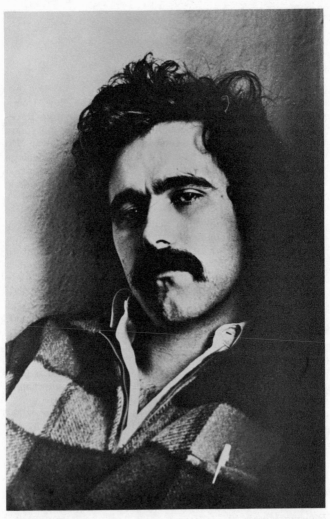

Ron Rice, a wild and talented man with a camera, died almost before he could get started.

The title of Rice's *The Flower Thief* comes from the scene in the film where Taylor Mead steals a flower, then sniffs it.

some money, and the next morning Rice left by jet for Mexico, never completing the film.

Returning again to New York, he made *Chumlum* (1964), an Arabian Nights vision of a palace brothel, inspired by Jerry Joffen and Jack Smith. In it gorgeously costumed characters, surrounded by diaphanous draperies, fumble through vague and erotic acts in hammocks. Much use is made of superimpositions, creating a sensual flow of color and space, and over it all jangles an Angus MacLise sound track.

Rice went back to Mexico. He did some shooting on a new film, but was unable to develop much of what he had shot or to get more raw stock. He had no money. In December he was admitted to a hospital in Acapulco and died there of bronchial pneumonia. He left behind lavish notes, plans for many films, and a wife and a child.

Rice was an extravagant personality. He was brash enough to write a letter to Joe Levine demanding support. He was strong enough to go for days and days without sleep. His notes are filled with fantastic scenes and descriptions. When he died, many film-makers felt it was a case of not enough money to make films, not enough money to live. Perhaps, however, it was his continued use of drugs that broke his health. His vision in film was too extravagant for simple continuity and basic technique. Possibly his vision of life was too extravagant to live.

Harry Smith
Born 1923, Portland, Oregon
Lives New York, New York

Harry Smith has been a painter, a student, a heroin addict, and an alchemist, and he has utilized all these activities in his work.

He defines his films thus:

> My cinematic excretia is of four varieties: batiked abstractions made directly on film between 1939 and 1946; optically printed nonobjective studies composed around 1950; semirealistic animated collages made as part of my alchemical labors of 1957 to 1962; and chronologically superimposed photographs of actualities formed since the

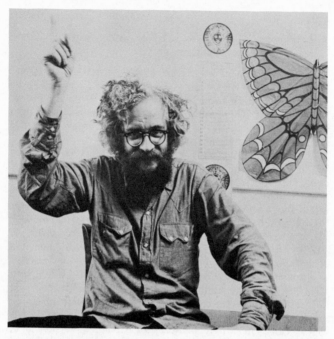

Harry Smith gestures jestingly, but nobody ever knows what is tumbling about in his madman mind. (*John Palmer*)

latter year . . . they are valuable works, works that will live forever—they made me gray.

Smith grew up in a deserted boomtown on Puget Sound in Washington. His parents were occultists, and when he was twelve, Smith began to learn alchemy from his father. He spent time while still a teen-ager with the Salish Indians working out methods of recording their ceremonies, later studied (and is still studying) anthropology.

He began making films while living in Berkeley and San Francisco, and roughly half of his film work has survived hotel fires and so on. He has collated the survivors by numbers. *Numbers 1* (1939), *2* (1940–42), and *3* (1942–47) are abstract films, painted on raw stock, possibly done later than Smith dates them, but completely original. They look like the sexual fantasies of a super-civilization. *4* (1950), *5* (1950), *6* (1951), and *7* (1951) were all optically printed except *No. 5*, a color abstraction. *No. 6* is three-dimensional.

Numbers 8 (1954), *9* (1954), *10* (1956), *11* (1956), and *12* (1943–58) are animated collage films. Smith used old illustrations in a surrealistic manner to act out imagined mystical adventures. The longest is *Number 12*, which Jonas Mekas calls *The Magic Feature*, an expanded version of *8*, which takes its materials from nineteenth-century ladies' wear catalogs and elocution books and turns them into terrifying apparitions on a strange journey.

Number 13 (1962) was a project to make a commercial animated version of *The Wizard of Oz*. It was to be a widescreen and stereophonic-sound production. A crew of twelve worked on it under Smith's direction until the major backer was found dead in a locked room. All that survives of this film are three hours of test shots. *Number 14* (1964–65) is a superimpositional film. *Number 15* (1965–66) features patterns of Seminole Indian art.

Smith has painted special screens for some films, and made special projectors with colored filters and supplementary slides for others. When not living in hotels, he is usually with the Indians, collecting sights, sounds, and artifacts. In occult circles he is considered a magician of some standing.

Jack Smith
Born 1932, Columbus, Ohio
Lives New York, New York

Jack Smith is an anarchist, and his films break all the rules of film art. They go too far, and they do it on purpose. They are too scratchy, too nervous, too vulgar, and at times, too beautiful. Thus his *Flaming Creatures* has become the only underground film banned in the State of New York. And when taken to Europe for the Third International Experimental Film Competition, it was replaced on the program with a note saying, "the selection jury . . . recognized the aesthetical and experimental qualities of the film *Flaming Creatures* by Jack Smith (U.S.A. 1963), but had to ascertain unanimously that the showing of it was impossible in regard to Belgian laws."

Smith peoples his films with "creatures," as he calls them, from the dark corners of society. He costumes these creatures in rags of moldy glory, and photographs them with a camera style that is torn between sloth and nervous irritability. Despite their anarchic appearance, his films are totally controlled with regard to framing and composition, and the mood of each film is usually essayed ahead of time with a series of still photographs. This care is becoming more visible as his later films, such as *Normal Love,* become more spectacularly beautiful. Smith's emotional sensibility, however, remains on the other side of *Angst,* a smoldering and triumphant madness.

Smith came to New York in 1950 and began hanging around theatre groups. He studied dancing with Ruth St. Denis and later direction with Lee Strasberg. His first film, never completed, was *Buzzards over Baghdad* (1951–56). He then acted in the films of Ken Jacobs and others, and once put on with Jacobs a nightclub show in Provincetown, promptly closed by the police, called "The Human Wreckage Review." He made *Overstimulated* (1960) and then *Scotch Tape* (1961), which shows various creatures in medium long shot picking their way through a New Jersey dump.

His next film was *Flaming Creatures* (1962–63) with its strange personages, whose sex is certain only when their genitals are showing. It contains such scenes as a penis

This 1959 self-portrait by Jack Smith shows him, as he says, "listening to the laughing horse and dreaming of little boys."

creeping over someone's shoulder and ends with a combination earthquake and orgy. In giving Smith the Independent Film Award, Jonas Mekas wrote, "He has attained for the first time in motion pictures a high level of art which is absolutely lacking in decorum; and a treatment of sex which makes us aware of the restraint of all previous film-makers." *Flaming Creatures* was confiscated by the New York Police, and a legal battle is still being waged around it.

Smith began work on *The Great Pasty Triumph*, which became *Normal Love* (1963–). Much of it was photographed with out-dated color stock, and the resulting compositions in shades of green and pink are bizarre and pleasing. The characters, including the Pink Fairy, The Mummy, The Spider, and a mermaid bathing in a pool of milk, have horror and fantasy ancestries. Final editing is not complete.

For the New Cinema Festival, he did a play, *Rehearsal for the Destruction of Atlantis* (1965), which he describes as "a political play that takes place in a child's vegetable garden of foreign policy cadavers." The audience is blindfolded before entering the theatre, and having taken their blindfolds off at the beginning of the play, they are told at the end, by The Lobster who is the hero, to put their blindfolds on and to get out.

Following this, Smith shot forty-five minutes of color of the Carnival in Brazil to be used in a commercial documentary. Currently he is making *In the Grip of the Lobster* (1966–), in color, presumably of further adventures of The Lobster in what Smith calls "The Lobster Age."

Smith is one of the major stars of underground films. His essays appear in *Film Culture*, and Piero Heliczer collected his early photographs in *The Beautiful Book*.

He lives in a two-floor loft, with half of the middle floor removed for filming from above. He has had many run-ins with the law, the most recent when he struck a Federal narcotics agent who was raiding a poetry reading.

Stan VanDerBeek
Born 1931, New York, New York
Lives Stony Point, New York.

Stan VanDerBeek is the Tom Swift of the underground, an inventor of processes and approaches. He is also a collagist, a collisionist, and like George Méliès, whom he claims as godfather, an illusionist. His earliest films, such as *What Who How*, are animated collages, his midway films, such as *Breathdeath*, are collages of film technique, and his latest works, including the environmental Movie-Drome, are collages of media.

He is a collisionist because he likes to bring disparate elements together at high speed, cut-outs of cars, pictures of politicians, pin-ups from *Playboy*, and so on, and give them some new meaning in the resulting crash. He is an illusionist because everything in his films is always changing into something else, cars into carnivorous creatures, hands into birds, and so on. The tone of his films has always been blackly humorous, and increasingly there have appeared overtones of social comment.

VanDerBeek graduated from a science high school in New York and went for a short while to Cooper Union to study architecture. In 1952 he went to the Black Mountain School of Art, not going to classes, but tending the school farm and working on painting and calligraphy. He had the use of a camera there, and so made "mythical" movies with a group of dancers. These movies were planned, performed, and photographed, except that there was no film in the camera. Nobody could afford film.

For two years following Black Mountain, he made flip books. Then he got a job doing backgrounds for a children's television program called *Winky Dink and You*. Part of the program's equipment was an animation stand and camera. VanDerBeek would come back late at night and tell the night watchman he had some work to do and would then use the camera and stand to make his first films. He was fired after six months (for being non-union) but continued for a year after that to return to the studio at night to tell the watchman he had late work to do. In this eighteen-month period he made *What Who How* (1955) and *Visioniii*

(1955), both animated collages, plus four unnamed studies (1955–56) that involved both collages and time paintings. Later he made *Mankinda* (1956–57), which was a time painting, that is, a painting seen happening as it happens, combined with a poem and calligraphy. And he continued his collage animation work with *Yet* (1957), *Street Meet* (1957), *Astral Man* (1958), and *Ala Mode* (1958).

By 1958 he was set up with techniques and facilities and began photographing vast amounts of material, usually shooting much footage around a particular idea. Then he would just "slice a film off like a sausage." He is still editing this material. Out of it has come *Wheeels #2* (1958–59), *Wheeels # 1* (1958–61), *Wheeels # 4* (1958–65), *Dance of the Looney Spoons* (1958–65), *Revenge of the Looney Spoons* (1958–65), and *Science Friction* (1958–65). He also worked at this time on a prototype for his later expanded-cinema presentations, *Three-Screen-Scene* (1958). In all of these films he used illustrations from magazines and advertisements for collage materials, making the inanimate animate, the large appear small, one object turn out to be another object, and so on.

His next step was to develop an apparatus that allowed him to combine live footage and collage animation, synchronized, on one film. His first such film was *Achoo Mr. Kerroochev* (1960), in which a cut-out of Nikita Khrushchev sailed over various newsreel events as they took place. This process became standard with many animated VanDerBeek films, including *Skullduggery Part I* (1960) and *Part II* (1960–61). Certain footage, such as a subjective view of a bare bosomed lady making a landing on an aircraft carrier, was used in several films. At the same time, too, he made *Black and Whites, Days and Nights* (1960), an animated cartoon of line drawings over a sound track of dirty limericks.

VanDerBeek also began to do live-action photography. He shot a large amount of footage recording Happenings by Claes Oldenburg and Allen Kaprow. The only work edited so far from this is the short *Snapshots of the City* (1961), of an Oldenburg work. He made the slapstick *Croquet Quacks* (1962–   ), and *Summit* (1963). *Summit*, a political satire on a meeting between Khrushchev and Kennedy, featured another technique, one possibly not used since Len Lye was animating in England, the manipulation of live actors with

The Madonna blasts off in VanDerBeek's *Science Friction*.
(*Collection* Film Quarterly)

an optical printer. This allowed VanDerBeek to orchestrate their movements and to cause comical reverses of action and so on.

Breathdeath (1963–64) is VanDerBeek's most ambitious single-projector film. It is an antiwar film dedicated to Buster Keaton and Charlie Chaplin, and a compendium of VanDer-Beek technique to that moment. It has scenes such as a picture of Richard Nixon with a foot suddenly coming out of his mouth, people dancing with little skeleton heads animated over their faces, a time painting painted on his wife's face, and blood pouring over a newspaper full of hydrogen bomb headlines.

In 1964 VanDerBeek received a Ford Foundation grant and, while working on his older style *A Damn Rib Bed* (1964–65), began to branch out. Given an animation camera with which it was possible to make dissolves, he made three films that were essentially loops, starting in one place, dissolving through a series of transformations, and dissolving back to that original place. These included *See Saw Seems* (1965–66), *If You Say So* (1965–66), and *Snow Show* (1965–66). He made an animated line loop in 35mm, called *Night Eating* (1965), reduced it to 8mm and made a cartridge out of it for tiny portable projectors. He made *Fluids* (1965), and *Phenomena* (1965), which used several layers of "zip tone" in motion to create optical patterns. He produced the simple *Facescapes* (1965) and *The Human Face Is a Monument* (1965), the content indicated by the titles. He made *The Life and Death of a Car* (1962–) and *Kar Bop* (1962–), which added live action of cars in motion, photographed with a special 180-degree distortion lens, to previously shot footage.

He was at this time becoming more and more involved with expanded cinema and working as an adjunct to dance works. For a Merce Cunningham dance piece, he made the three-screen *Variation 5* (1965), which included shots of Cunningham dancing, the astronauts floating in space, and Nam June Paik's electronic television distortions. He did *Sight* (1965) for a Bob Morris dance work, and photographed Yvonne Rainer's *Room Service* (1965). He made *Pastorale: Et Al* (1965), which is photographed portions of a dance combined with a dance by dancers carrying little

This scene from *Facescapes* reveals some of VanDerBeek's technique with collage.

Stan VanDerBeek poses before his Movie-Drome during its construction in the hills of Stony Point, New York. (*Lenny Lipton*)

movie screens, on which is projected the film dance, this done
by Elaine Summers and Bert Supree.

VanDerBeek has been especially involved with multiple
projection pieces. He calls them "movie-murals" and "newsreels of dreams." They were done in anticipation of the dome
he built at his home in Stony Point, the Movie-Drome, an
environmental movie theatre with all surfaces to be covered
by projected images. He put on his first multiple-screen
presentations at the New Cinema Festival in 1965, at the
Film-makers' Cinematheque. One was *Move-Movies* (1965),
a "choreography for projectors" in which there were two
projectors facing the stage, plus five portable projectors being
carried around the theatre by assistants. Parts of the work
were shown on the audience itself. Another was *Feedback
1* (1965), which used five slide and motion picture
projectors and two sound tracks in a sort of movie mix.

VanDerBeek's movie-murals are part of a plan to develop
a new visual language that could be used to communicate
broad concepts of existence among all the cultures of the
world. He calls this plan *Culture Intercom* and wants all the
governments of the world to build movie-dromes like his
own, to connect these through satellite television stations,
and to allow them to exchange "images" so as to speed communication between cultures and to bring them some better
and more immediate understanding of themselves and of
each other. He sees a race between world destruction and
world communication, with the lack of the latter accelerating
the former.

VanDerBeek is presently editing a live-action film of country hi-jinks by Claes Oldenburg and crew, *Birth of the
American Flag* (1965–   ). He has done for CBS "an electronic collage" with videotape called *Panels for the Walls of
the World # 1* (1965). He has also made two computer-
generated films, *Collide-oscope* (1966) and *When in the
Course of* (1966–   ).

He has continued with various other activities while his
film work has remained central, and a recent exhibition of
his work listed the following: calligraphy, stills, paintings,
polaroid constructions, sculpture, rollings, wooden boxes, and
collages. He is also interested in architecture, having built
both his house and the Movie-Drome.

Andy Warhol
Born 1928, Newport, Rhode Island
Lives New York, New York

Most publicized of the recent underground films are the works of Andy Warhol. They are films that seem to show a world of silvery living death, and some of them, such as *Sleep*, are movies that do not move—almost. All are precariously balanced between the controlled and the casual.

So carefully static that the slightest variance in exposure, framing, or on-screen movement can jolt the sensibilities, these neodocumentaries were meant to get attention. They did. They also showed to what degree a movie could be reduced and still be a movie.

There are roughly four periods in Andy Warhol's film work. The well-known first period productions, such as *Sleep*, are classically simple films, slow paced and silent, with harsh lighting and no drama. Second period films, such as *The Life of Juanita Castro*, are poetic and satiric dramas, and are, with sound and more complex staging, less blandly pure. Third period films, such as *Beauty Number 2*, while still using an immobile camera, are realistic *cinéma vérité*-style dramas, some with conventional lighting. The fourth period is Warhol's work with "expanded cinema," and includes his work with live performance groups and *The Chelsea Girls*.

Warhol is primarily a visual stylist. Although many people work on his films, even to the extent of writing and directing them, he exerts final control by choice of subject matter and visual approach. Thus, no matter who writes it, who photographs it, who appears in it, or who directs it, an Andy Warhol film is unmistakable. In fact, his combined films might be considered as being part of one huge work, the definitive documentary on the socialites, starlets, addicts, homosexuals, fashion models, artists, and people-on-the-make who comprise New York's bizarre *demi-monde*.

After graduating in art in 1950 from the Carnegie Institute, Warhol became first a leading New York fashion illustrator, then the pop artist who painted soup cans. In the spring of 1963 he bought a movie camera. He experimented with flash frame films, and on a trip to Hollywood, made *Tarzan and Jane Regained . . . Sort of* (1963).

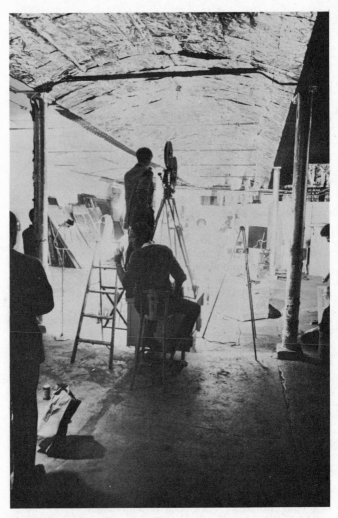

Andy Warhol ponders the action taking place in his silvery film studio as he wraps up his *Vinyl* in one take. (*David McCabe*)

The film that launched Warhol's now famous first period style was *Sleep* (1963), which shows a man sleeping for six hours. (It is actually three hours of ten-minute segments that were shot over a six-week period. Each segment is shown twice.)

Warhol's method is to make many films and publicize the few that are good. The bad are shown once, and sometimes their titles are used again on other attempts. The following are those on record as having followed *Sleep*.

Eat (1963); *Kiss* (1964); *Naomi and Rufus Kiss* (1964); *Haircut* (1964); *Roller Skate* (1964); *Dance Movie* (1964); *Salome and Delilah* (1964); *Pause* (1964); *Apple* (1964); *Messy Lives* (1964); *The End of Dawn* (1964); *Lips* (1964); *Couch* (1964); *Empire* (1964), made with John Palmer; *The Thirteen Most Beautiful Women* (1964) and *The Thirteen Most Beautiful Boys* (1964); *Batman* (1964); *Shoulder* (1964); *The Lester Persky Story—A Soap Opera* (1964); *Henry Geldzahler* (1964); and *Blow Job* (1964).

Despite its perverse subject, *Blow Job* is one of the best examples of this period. It shows the head and shoulders of a man as a sexual act is allegedly being performed on him. In forty minutes' time, his face, interrupted only by the white-out of exposed reel endings, goes through a long ecstasy. The starkly lit head moving back and forth under light and shadow builds up a strong sense of volume without editing, tells a story without words, camera movement, or montage.

Harlot (1965), Warhol's version of *Harlow*, with female impersonator Mario Montez as the star, and *Drunk* (1965), began his sound era and ended his first period.

The second period is mainly dramas written by Ronald Tavel. These include *Screen Test Number One* (1965); *Screen Test Number Two* (1965); the stagey *Life of Juanita Castro* (1965); and *Vinyl* (1965), which features an interior documentary on sadism. Seen less often are *Suicide* (1965); *Horse* (1965); *Bitch* (1965); and *Kitchen* (1965), all marred by minor technical disasters.

Third period direction and scenarios were provided by Chuck Wein. Among these are *Beauty Number Two* (1965), about a confused pseudosexual *ménage à trois*; *Prison* (1965); various segments built around Edie Sedgwick called *Poor Little Rich Girl* (1965); and *My Hustler* (1965), a

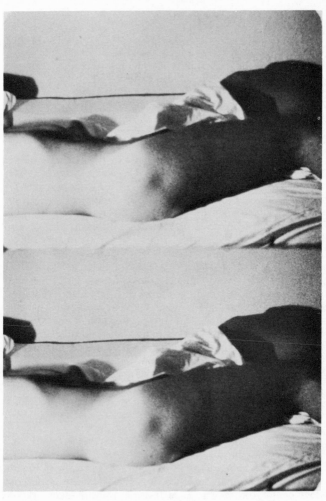

Actually a johnny-come-lately to the underground film scene, Warhol's *Sleep*, first of his films to gain wide attention, was made in 1963.

sharkish semidocumentary on homosexual prostitutes. At the same time, Warhol made *Space* (1965) and some videotape experiments.

After a variety film of "camp" people and routines called *Camp* (1965), Warhol began showing split-screen presentations. They were mostly half-hour takes not interesting enough to be shown by themselves and so converted into simultaneous double features. Films shot around this time include *Whips* (1966), *Faces* (1966), *More Milk Yvette* (1966), *Hedy (The Fourteen Year Old Girl)* (1966), numerous Edie Sedgwick reels, and *The Bed* (1966). Shown first in a presentation called *Up Tight*, with a rock and roll group named The Velvet Underground, his live/film presentation eventually became *The Exploding Plastic Inevitable*, a discotheque environment in which the split screen productions were projected over the bands and dancers.

Warhol culled the best from a series of half-hour takes photographed at the Hotel Chelsea and combined them into the three-and-a-half-hour-long *The Chelsea Girls* (1966), which actually used seven hours of material, three and a half on each side of the screen.

Warhol produces most of his films in a loft lined with silver paint and foil called "The Factory." His flair for publicity is considerable, and of the underground people he is the most often visible. He has also helped make celebrities of a sort of his "superstars," Naomi Levine, Baby Jane Holzer, Edie Sedgwick, and Nico.

FOUR: Stars of
the Underground Films

There is not much emphasis in underground films on "stars." For one thing, it is the film-maker himself who is in the underground limelight. For another, most underground works are not narratives and hence do not use featured players.

People appear in underground films, of course, but those that stand out are the ones who communicate a powerful sense of *personality* on film, and not those who act well. These "stars" are people who communicate this sense of personality despite the visual pyrotechnics of camera work and editing that is going on around their presence. And they must be able to communicate this sense without the aid of professional make-up, custom costumes, or careful lighting set-ups.

Even to be in these films, the underground star must be willing to work without pay. He must be willing to put in the time even though he knows the resulting film may never be seen, or even developed. He must be available to appear whenever the film-maker is shooting. And he must be "on Scene" in order to know the various film-makers, for needless to say, there is no underground Central Casting Agency. And this explains why most of the actors and actresses listed here are film-makers themselves.

Jack Smith

Jack Smith is better known for his appearances in other people's work than for his own films. He looks like Punch of Punch and Judy, and also like a thin, tall, hairy Peter Ustinov. In one film he pulls a baby face and stares the camera down. In another he chews the crotch of a rubber doll with satanic glee. And in another he floats gowned across the screen in a transvestite trance.

Smith started as some kind of passionate gypsy lady dancing down stairs in Ken Jacobs's *Little Cobra Dance: Saturday Afternoon Blood Sacrifice*, also acting in Jacobs's *Little Stabs at Happiness, Blonde Cobra, The Death of P'Town* and *Star Spangled to Death*. For Ron Rice he acted in *Chumlum* and *The Queen of Sheba Meets the Atom Man*, and for George Kuchar in the 8mm *The Lovers of Eternity*.

Smith's favorite role was as Andy Warhol's *Batman*, and he appeared in Warhol's *Camp*. He is in Bill Vehr's *The Mysterious Spanish Lady* and *Brothel*. And on a trip to San Francisco, he acted in Carl Linder's *Skin* and *The Devil Is Dead*. He played the title role of Dov Lederberg's *Eargogh*. He is in Markopoulos's *The Illiac Passion* and Naomi Levine's *Jeremelu* and Piero Heliczer's *Dirt*. And add to his credits unnamed films by Jerry Joffen.

Taylor Mead

Taylor Mead looks like a cross between a kewpie doll and Fred Astaire gone bad. He is a natural mime who lackadaisically underplays, even when "camping it up."

Ron Rice and Vernon Zimmerman met him at a poetry reading in San Francisco, and both put him in their first films. In Rice's *The Flower Thief*, Mead plays a passive beatnik, stealing flowers, riding down a hill on a wagon, and appearing in mock melodramas. In Zimmerman's *Lemon Hearts* (1960–61), he does all the parts, eleven different characters, even proposing marriage to himself in one scene. Zimmerman later used him in a satire on Hollywood called *To L.A. . . . With Lust* (1961–62), and Mead had the main role in Rice's never completed *Queen of Sheba Meets the Atom Man*. Mead also appeared, while in San Francisco, in

Jack Smith stands in bedecked glory in Ken Jacobs's *Star Spangled to Death.*

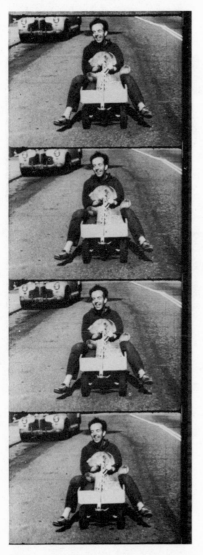

Taylor Mead and teddy bear cruise down a San Francisco hill in *The Flower Thief*.

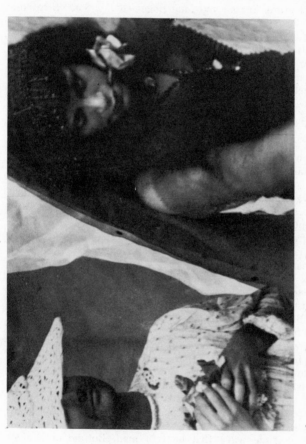

Mario Montez, known as Dolores Flores at the time, appears in Jack Smith's *Flaming Creatures* dancing a fandango with a rose between his/her teeth.

two 8mm films by Bob Chatterton, *The Hobo and The Circus* and *Passion in a Seaside Slum*.

When Andy Warhol came west with Naomi Levine in 1963, Mead went back into production as Tarzan in Warhol's first feature, *Tarzan and Jane Regained . . . Sort of.* In New York he appeared in Paul Morrisey's *Taylor Mead Dances* (1963), doing an imaginary strip tease with tin cans tied to his legs. He then appeared in two semicommercial films, *Open the Door and See All the People* (1964) and Robert Downey's *Babo 73* (1964). In Hill's film he played a garbage collector. In Downey's he was the President of the United States. Brendan Gill in *The New Yorker* noted that he spoke "as if his mind and mouth were full of marshmallow."

Mario Montez

Mario Montez was discovered, as they say, by Jack Smith in a subway station. His name was not then Mario Montez. It was something else, and for *Flaming Creatures* it was Dolores Flores. Mario has played women in all his films except Robert Blossom's pseudopornographic *Movie.* When he dresses up, he undergoes a metamorphosis into a dizzy and vain young thing. He acts like a woman. He looks like a woman. His fantasy is very real.

He appears as a mermaid bathing in milk in Jack Smith's *Normal Love* and is in Smith's *In the Grip of the Lobster.* He is in Rice's *Chumlum*, José Rodriguez-Soltero's *Lupita*, and Bill Vehr's *The Mystery of the Spanish Lady, Lil Picards, Beauty Environment of the Year 2065*, and *Brothel.*

Montez has also been one of Warhol's stable of stars, playing Jean Harlow in *Harlot*, Lana Turner in *More Milk, Yvette*, and Hedy Lamarr in *The Fourteen Year Old Girl.* He is in *Camp*, and his most touching performance is in Warhol/Tavel's *Screen Test Number Two.* There he plays an actress auditioning for a part, and in the end he is completely humiliated by being forced to admit (in the most basic possible way) that he is a man. But he only gives way and admits this humiliation because he is a woman.

Naomi Levine

Naomi Levine is the buxom queen of the underground. She started as a monster character, "The Spider," in Smith's *Normal Love*, where she was discovered by Andy Warhol. Warhol made her his first superstar with *Tarzan and Jane Regained . . . Sort of*, followed by *Kiss, Naomi and Rufus Kiss, Couch, Dracula*, and *Soap Opera*.

She was in Barbara Rubin's *Christmas on Earth*, Ken Jacobs's 8mm *Naomi Is a Vision of Loveliness*, and Jerry Joffen's films. She also did a bit for Jonas Mekas's film diary in which she wrapped herself in an American flag and rolled down a snowy street.

Naomi Levine was originally a painter, and she has made films as well, including the unique pastorale *Yes* (1964), and *Jeremelu* (1965), which is a rapid montage of flowers and young men's anatomy.

Gerard Malanga

Gerard Malanga is a poet. He is also Andy Warhol's right-hand man and not surprisingly has ended up in many Warhol movies. He communicates on film an air of arrogance that is accentuated by a strange combination of "beautiful boy" and "tough guy" affectations. His best film is probably *Vinyl*, the sado-masochist Warhol film that Ronald Tavel wrote especially for him.

He has been in these other Warhol films: *Camp, Harlot, Kiss, Couch, Assassination, The Thirteen Most Beautiful Boys, Soap Opera, The Gerard Malanga* section of *The Chelsea Girls*, and certain films used in *The Exploding Plastic Inevitable* show. He appears in Marie Menken's *Andy Warhol*.

He is also in Barbara Rubin's *Christmas on Earth*, Piero Heliczer's 8mm *Dirt* and *Joan of Arc*, Smith's *Normal Love*, Rice's *Chumlum*, Markopoulos's *The Illiac Passion* and Levine's *Jeremelu*. He plays the romantic lead in Andrew Meyer's *Match Girl* (1964), and has most recently appeared in Warren Sonbert's *Hall of Mirrors* (1966).

Malanga has also made his own films, among them *Academy Leader* (1964), *Son of Academy Leader* (1966), A

The young hood in *Vinyl* is Gerard Malanga, and the girl is
Edie Sedgwick, only a Warhol starlet at the time.

Private Moment (1966), *Cambridge Diary* (1966), and many others.

Claes Oldenburg

Claes Oldenburg's stardom has been an outgrowth of his role as maker and performer of Happenings. People film the Happenings, and there he is. This is not to say that he does not enjoy participating in films. From 1960 there have always been special performances of his events for film-makers to shoot.

While he is gaunt looking and nervous in person, he appears on the screen to be bearlike and deliberate. He performs acts of wild absurdity with total deadpan. He is the fifth Marx Brother.

VanDerBeek's *Snapshots of the City* was the first work to be made from his Happenings, and Oldenburg assisted on the making of the sound track. After that came a sort of pop art farce in the country made by Robert Breer. It included the complete Oldenburg entourage and was called *Pat's Birthday*. Vernon Zimmerman turned Oldenburg's *Gayety* happening into *Scarface and Aphrodite* (1963), and Raymond Saroff has made many film records of his Happenings, including the two compilation films, *Happenings I* and *II* (1962–64).

A British artist, John Jones, made *Claes Oldenburg Hangs a Picture* (1966), and VanDerBeek's *Birth of the American Flag*, showing wild goings-on on a country weekend, is being edited. There remain, too, immense amounts of unedited footage of his Happenings, photographed by many different film-makers.

Oldenburg has done a Happening called *Moviehouse* (1965), which orchestrates the characters and events in movie audiences. It is the result of his idea that the movie is not going on on the screen, but in the movie theatre.

Pat Oldenburg, Claes's wife, appears in almost all of the above films.

Others

Many have starred in underground films, but usually only in those of one film-maker. Andy Warhol especially has had

Claes Oldenburg stirs in a bucket, his wife Pat dances, and a man writes nonsequiturs on a blackboard in this moment from an Oldenburg Happening, as shown in Vernon Zimmerman's *Scarface and Aphrodite*.

a succession of "superstars," as he calls them, including the petite Edie Sedgwick, the tall and lanky Baby Jane Holzer, and Nico, who had previously been in *La Dolce Vita* and in exploitation films. Warhol himself shows up in many films by other film-makers.

And one should not forget Marie Menken. She is the underground's main character actress. She started by appearing in her husband Willard Maas's films. She was the prostitute for whom Jack Smith cuts off his ear in Lederberg's *Eargogh*. She played the title role in Tavel/Warhol's *The Life of Juanita Castro* and is in other Warhol films, including *Prison* and *The Chelsea Girls*. Menken is also part of the chorus in Charles Boultenhouse's *Dionysus* (1963).

FIVE: The Underground Establishment

Exhibition, distribution, and critical notice are powerful factors in deciding which films get made, which get seen, and which become well known. In underground films, as in commercial films, the fate of a particular work may rest more on the elements of business and publicity than on a film's actual virtue.

The number of underground films made and seen in the past few years has multiplied immensely. This has been both the cause and the result of business involvement by the film-makers themselves.

The Film Establishment

An important fact was discovered about film almost as soon as the medium was invented: people are so attracted to certain forms of film that they will pay to see them. Thus the film medium has, from its beginnings, been used to make money. It is also a fact that films are expensive to make. Films have had to make money to pay for their production cost.

Almost all films, including documentaries, educational films, propaganda films, entertainment films, and those of the variety sometimes called "art films," have been commercial films. Until the personal film came along, all films, to get produced, had to have some potential financial worth. This meant the potential for film as art was unrealized, for only those innovations were pursued that could somehow lead to material profit.

Out of this long-term economic reality, there developed a solid structure of agreement about what film is and what it should be. This agreement is the basis for an invisible *film establishment* that encompasses nearly all film backers, film-makers, film audiences, and even film critics. All believe that every film should be entertaining, or at least educational. All believe that every film should make immediate sense, economically, visually, morally, and politically. In the long view, differences of opinion in the commercial film world have always been very slight.

The critics and the audiences have been exposed to little variation from formula films. And even the "art films" are bound by formulas of their own. When films of the complexity and the individuality of the underground variety come along, the critics and the audiences (at least average audiences) do not want to see them.

The commercial film establishment is so congealed that the work of the underground is essentially locked out. There are no facilities in this establishment for such films to be distributed, exhibited, or commented upon. Thus they have not been able to reach the audience that does exist for them.

The underground has done the only thing it could do without either having its films go unseen or making its films more conventional. The underground has formed its own establishment.

The Twenties

The films of the first avant-garde were exhibited in small art theatres around continental Europe and in the many *ciné* clubs, leagues, and societies that grew up with the interest inspired by the avant-garde. In the United States these films, and their few American counterparts, were shown in similar small theatres. But interest was limited and disappeared after the start of the Depression. An idea of how little interest there was is given by the amount of money Man Ray is said to have received for permanent American rights to his films—two hundred dollars.

It was not until 1937, when the Museum of Modern Art was distributing them, that the first avant-garde films began being seen again. The museum distributed to other museums,

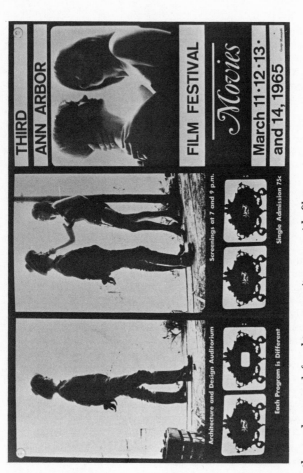

One way the underground fought anonymity was with film festivals such as this one at Ann Arbor. (*Jack Newman*)

to schools, and to nonprofit film societies. In doing so, it began to develop the major market for the coming experimental and underground films.

Builders of the Underground Establishment

The underground establishment is the result of pioneering attitudes and efforts by a few key people. The first of these was Maya Deren, who innovated the idea of extensive self-promotion by experimentalists themselves. Before her marriage to the man with whom she made *Meshes of the Afternoon*, Deren was secretary for the Katherine Dunham Dancers. After making films, and being unable to get satisfactory distribution or exhibition, she rented the Provincetown Playhouse in New York's Greenwich Village, and exhibited them herself. She also distributed her films from her own home, publicized them with articles and lectures, and set up the Creative Film Foundation to provide cash awards and production money for experimental films.

When the West Coast explosion of interest in experimental film took place, it was Frank Stauffacher's Art in Cinema exhibitions that served as its focal point. Stauffacher was a commercial artist with an interest in film. He organized, with Richard Foster, a series of annual exhibitions at the San Francisco Museum of Art. The first series took place in 1947 and, with a guiding hand from Hans Richter, included a massive review of avant-garde cinema up to that date. Although Art in Cinema eventually drifted away from experimental film, and then ended with the early death of Stauffacher in 1955, it was the first major renaissance in this country of avant-garde film, and its guarantee of a place of exhibition was enough to result in the production of many films.

Stauffacher made another important addition through Art in Cinema. His first program was actually a book that contained a collection of avant-garde history, film notes, essays, and photographs. This book was the only guide to such films for many years in this country. Its appearance accelerated interest in them, and not only in New York, but in such an unlikely place as Sweden.

The Art in Cinema book was one of the catalysts that

Panelists for an October, 1953, symposium on "Poetry and the Film" included (left to right) Dylan Thomas, Arthur Miller, Willard Maas, Parker Tyler, Amos Vogel, and Maya Deren. (*Collection Cinema 16*)

brought Amos Vogel to the founding of Cinema 16. As a boy in Vienna, Vogel had attended film society showings. Later, after escaping to America from Nazi Austria, he discovered he could not see the films he read about in Stauffacher's catalog and other places. Thus he followed Maya Deren's example, and began showing these films himself at the Provincetown Playhouse. By 1950 he had founded the Cinema 16 Film Library, the first distribution set-up devoted primarily to contemporary experimental films.

Cinema 16 exhibited films for sixteen years, succumbing in 1963 to rising exhibition costs; the distribution operation was sold to the Grove Press in 1966. Vogel helped found the Creative Film Foundation, and after leaving Cinema 16 to head the New York Film Festival, served to publicize American independent films by showing many of them at the festival.

Vogel introduced many of the early underground films, but it was Jonas Mekas, another immigrant from Europe, who became the central figure in promoting the underground. Mekas spent the first part of his life herding cows in a peasant village in Lithuania. After he finally got to go to school (at age fourteen), the Nazis invaded, and then the Russians. He and his brother Adolfas put out a series of underground resistance newspapers. Both brothers ended up in Nazi concentration camps, then lived for five years after the war in displaced persons camps. They came to America in 1950, and five years later Jonas started *Film Culture*, "America's Independent Motion Picture Magazine."

An early issue contained a somewhat critical article on experimental film-makers written by Mekas, but he soon changed his mind. Under his editorship *Film Culture* became the main source of comment and information on independent film-making of all kinds. Later he helped bring together independent film-makers of varying shades to form the New American Cinema Group. Their ideas of the film-makers' mutual support, exhibition, and distribution, originated by Maya Deren, were again put forth.

These ideas became a reality when Mekas started the Film-makers' Cooperative in 1962. At the same time he arranged for a series of exhibitions, starting with the famous Monday night showings at the Charles Theater, on New York's Lower East Side, to showcase the underground works

With a poet's passion and a peasant's shrewdness, Jonas
Mekas has helped lift personal film-making in America out
of The Abyss. (*Peter Saladino*)

that no one else would run. The Film-makers' Cinematheque, now operated as part of the Film Culture Non Profit Corporation, is the successor to the Charles. Mekas also forced censorship cases, worked to bring foundation money to the film-makers, kept the rest of the world informed through his weekly column in *The Village Voice*, and, incidentally, made films.

Mekas operates mainly in the environs of New York City, but there are many others working in parallel ways to promote the films. In the early sixties, John Fles took the films around Los Angeles, showing them to everybody who would look. In San Francisco, Bruce Baillie founded the Canyon Cinema organization, which has its own publication, and now its own cooperative distribution center. George Manupelli has exhibited the films in the Midwest out of his Ann Arbor headquarters. Together these individuals have built a new establishment to bring new kinds of films to a new audience. And while expanding the market for these films, they have devised methods of getting more and more money and help for the film-maker than ever before.

Exhibition

The major portion of avant-garde film exhibition has always been in museum, art center, and university film societies. It is not unusual to have, on larger campuses, a film society that specializes in showing avant-garde and underground films.

Another aspect of the growth of underground exhibition is the film-makers' showcases. These are the facilities that the film-makers set up when they cannot in other ways get their films shown to the public. The most famous is the Film-makers' Cinematheque in New York, which is now open every night of the week, having outlasted numerous censorship and licensing battles. The Canyon Cinema showcase used to show free films complete with free popcorn. It was closed by Berkeley authorities, only to pop up in another form in San Francisco. Regardless of their longevity, which is sometimes short, these facilities have continually brought the newest films out where people can see them. And the censorship fights that rage around them only serve to publicize the films more.

Film-makers' showcases have created and proven the interest in the newest films as they have emerged. Thus the films are increasingly being exhibited on a semicommercial basis by coffee houses, marginal theatres, and commercial "art houses." Sometimes they are shown on regular programs as shorts accompanying a feature. Sometimes they are shown at special midnight "matinees" on weekends. And recently a few of the films, *The Brig*, *Scorpio Rising*, and *The Chelsea Girls* have been shown as continuous features. In the case of *The Chelsea Girls*, no theatre would play it because of its length and the difficulty of the split-screen projection. Then the Film-makers' Distribution Center rented a mid-Manhattan movie theatre and did "standing room only" business for weeks. *The Chelsea Girls* has since become a remarkable commercial success, with an anticipated gross of over a million dollars.

A variation of the film-makers' showcase is the underground film festival, usually an annual affair with cash awards. These rarely last more than one or two years, but they do give exposure. The most durable of such festivals are George Manupelli's Ann Arbor Film Festival in Michigan and Foothill College's Independent Film-makers' Festival in California. Underground works also appear in the international festivals. *The Brig*, for example, won the documentary prize at Venice in 1964.

There are many variations on standard exhibition. There is the Fairchild Projector, for example, a self-contained unit that shows a film loop on a small screen that hides the projector. These little "movie boxes" were used to show the films of Robert Breer at the Bonino Gallery in New York and also Andy Warhol's work in the lobby of Philharmonic Hall during the New York Film Festival. And in Paris, Breer once soaped the front window of an art gallery and projected a film on it so that it could be seen by passers-by on the street.

The Film-makers' Cooperative now has a plan to sell 8mm reduction prints of underground films in book stores. They would be for people to take home, show to themselves, and own as they own books. Bruce Conner has already marketed 8mm versions of his films, selling for five and ten dollars apiece.

Distribution

There have always been two problems in the distribution of avant-garde/experimental/underground films. One has been the problem of getting distributed at all, and the other has been that of getting any significant financial return for the trouble. Originally the market for such films was almost nonexistent. And the profit on short-film rentals has always been diminutive. (It costs the same to handle a short as it does to handle a feature, but a short rents for only ten to fifty percent of what a feature rents for.)

The first extensive distribution of avant-garde films, by the Museum of Modern Art, was a nonprofit endeavor, with no return going to the original film-makers. Toward the end of the forties, a few of the experimentalists had their films distributed by Brandon Films and by Rosaland Kossoff (of Film Images, Inc.). Vogel's Cinema 16 Film Library, founded in 1950, was the first outlet to specialize in contemporary experimentalists. From 1951 to 1957 there was Kinesis, started by Brant Sloan and continued by Robert Greensfelder. And from 1958 there has been Robert Pike's Creative Film Society.

The film-maker usually entered into a contract with these organizations whereby he received fifty percent of the rental, after the cost of making the print had been recouped. In some cases the print was the property of the distributor, and in some cases it was the property of the film-maker. In the case of the Creative Film Society, the distributor paid three or four times the cost of the print to the film-maker, but did not pay any of the rental to him.

Distribution through these outlets had its disadvantages, however, for usually the distributor (Creative Film Society excepted) demanded an exclusive contract. And the distributors would distribute only those films they believed would make some money at least. This meant that if a film was too new or too different, it could not be distributed, a situation which was publicized when no one would show or distribute Stan Brakhage's *Anticipation of the Night*.

Therefore the Film-makers' Cooperative was founded. The Cooperative set a policy of distributing any film submitted to it. It let the film-maker set his own rental rate. It encouraged the film-maker to place his film with as many different rental outlets as possible, on the theory that the more available a film is, the more revenue it will return to its maker. The Cooperative paid seventy-five percent of the rental to the film-maker. But the film-maker had to provide the print.

The success of the Film-makers' Cooperative is reflected in the fact that it has now been joined by a London Cooperative, a Canyon Cinema Cooperative in San Francisco, and similar operations elsewhere, all working along the same lines. It has begun to break down the concept of exclusivity in the distribution of independent films. And it has resulted in an increase in the revenue from film rentals to the point where the better-known members of the underground can at least begin to live on their film-making.

In response to the increasingly commercial exhibition of underground films, the New York Cooperative has sprouted the Film-makers' Distribution Center. This organization, like the Cooperative, a part of The New American Cinema, Inc., markets feature-length independent films and film programs to commercial theatres. It is more aggressive in its promotion, and it takes a bigger bite from the return. But the film-maker still gets fifty percent of the gross revenue, where he would probably receive that percent of only the net revenue from a commercial distributor.

Financing

In discussing the business of the underground, one should not forget the question of how production money is raised, for the source of the money often dictates how it is to be used. Hollywood films are backed not by the studios, but by the banks, who finance the studio productions, but only after estimating the earning power of each production. American independent features, such as Shirley Clarke's *The Cool World*, are backed by a number of private investors, who often don't expect to recover their investment.

Underground films are backed by the same people who back painting and poems. And that is primarily the artist, his family, and his close friends. Recently the Ford, Rockefeller, and John Simon Guggenheim Foundations have given support to film-makers of already established reputation. Some film-makers have received small but strategically helpful checks in the mail from an organization identified only as "Friends of New Cinema." Robert Nelson received a check for $2500 in a box of jelly beans, sent by a woman in Pennsylvania who admired his films. Bruce Baillie used to borrow his production money from a friendly banker.

A Hollywood film costs from $200,000 to $20,000,000. An independent feature can cost from $40,000 to $100,000. John Cassavetes's *Shadows*, made in 1957, startled everybody with its low production cost of $14,000. Underground films, even underground features, cost much less.

In 1928 it cost just ninety-seven dollars to make Vorkapich and Florey's classic experimental film *Life and Death of 9413—A Hollywood Extra*. And in 35mm, too. (Several years later Roger Barlow is said to have made a short 35mm film for a total of four dollars. He did it by getting leftover film from the Hollywood studios and using every bit of it.) Cadged film is one of the economic shortcuts underground film-makers use. Out-of-date film stock, home developing, communal use of equipment and labor are others.

Animated films are the most inexpensive to make. Robert Breer says his films cost no more than home movies do. (And, of course, some underground films *are* home movies.) D'Avino's *A Trip* cost twenty-five dollars, complete with sound track. Warhol's hour-long sound films usually cost less than three hundred dollars apiece, but Warhol does no titling and no editing. Kaye's *Georg* and Goldman's *Echoes of Silence*, both with editing and sound tracks added later, cost about $1700 each.

Most film-makers, as they go along, become more and more technical perfectionists. This perfectionism results in a corresponding rise in production cost, which is sometimes balanced by greater experience in knowing where to cut corners and where not to. Still, the cost goes up. Anger's *Fireworks* was produced for approximately fifty dollars. His *Scorpio Rising* cost as much as $7000. And the planned *Lucifer Rising*, twenty years after *Fireworks*, is budgeted at $20,000.

Publications and Criticism

Even when underground films are shown publicly, newspapers and magazines skip mention of them almost com-

The Village Voice, Film Culture, and *Canyon Cinema News* are the places where most commentary on the underground appears. (*Jack Newman*)

pletely. Underground films are too complex and too personal; not spectacular and not inhibited enough for the people who write about commercial films. It has thus been necessary for the underground to have its own press.

Film Culture is the prime source of writing on the underground. A quarterly, it publishes not only articles and interviews, but stills and filmographies, as well as personal letters by the film-makers, their poems, their drawings, and their notes. Considerable space is devoted to historical coverage of film, too, as with the special D. W. Griffith issue.

Canyon Cinema News, a mimeographed monthly, is filled with film-making gossip from around the country. It contains a listing of current film festivals, and of most underground and museum showings. It also lists sources of inexpensive raw film stock, used equipment, and other cost cutters.

P. Adams Sitney has put out four issues of *Film Wise*, each an important compilation of material on a particular film-maker. Brakhage, Markopoulos, Deren, and a combination of Maas and Menken have been covered so far. Mention of the underground often appears in *Film Quarterly*, in a journal called *December*, in Mekas's column in *The Village Voice*, and in the numerous maverick weekly newspapers that are springing up around the country. (The press service that links these new weeklies is "The Underground Press Service.")

There are few underground film critics. The general scene is still too new and too confused. It is constantly being roiled by ever newer and more different kinds of films. Most writing on the film takes the form of appreciation pieces by friends of the film-makers, or comments by the film-makers themselves. Considering the personal nature of many of the films, this is not surprising.

The most influential of the underground critics is, of course, Jonas Mekas. He writes to explain, to excite, and sometimes to hurl a brickbat. A typical brickbat, hurled in his *Village Voice* column, after the City of New York confiscated films for being obscene, goes like this: "So the City is clubbing the arts again! So they are burning the books again, so they are tearing apart the little strips of film and the white blood of celluloid is drying in the impersonal and cold-eyed offices of the City . . ." Lest one be put off by his passionate tone, it should be noted that in his early writing in *Film Culture* he wrote with the precision and rationality of a college professor.

P. Adams Sitney and Ken Kelman are the only other consistently prolific writers on the subject. Sitney has been writing his intense analyses since he was in high school. In addition to publishing *Film Wise*, he edited Brakhage's *Metaphors on Vision*. Kelman is more critical than Mekas or Sitney. His writing is as complicated as Sitney's but is filled with double-edged wit.

The main historian, in English, of the first film avant-garde has so far been Hans Richter. Lewis Jacobs has written a brief history of the American film avant-garde up to 1946. And the resident critic of Cinema 16 and the experimental film period was Parker Tyler.*

Exporting the Underground

Europe did not get a look at personal art films by Americans until the 1958 Brussels Experimental Film Competition, held during the Brussels World's Fair. Brakhage was invited to show a retrospective. Belson and Henry Jacobs presented a *Vortex Concert*. Films by Len Lye, Hillary Harris, Hy Hirsch, and Brakhage won awards.

As a project of the New American Cinema Group, David Stone took fifty-four independent productions to the 1961 Festival of Two Worlds in Spoleto, Italy. These included everything from features such as Curtis Harrington's *Night Tide* and Rogosin's *On the Bowery* to the work of VanDer-Beek, Brakhage, Breer, and Markopoulos.

The real underground assault on Europe took place in 1963 and 1964 with the forming of the International Exposition of the New American Cinema. First presented by Mekas at the Third Brussels Experimental Film Competition, and then shown in museums and schools all around Europe by P. Adams Sitney, this selection of underground work received unbelievable publicity and caused not a few student riots.

* *The New American Cinema: A Critical Anthology*, edited by Gregory Battcock (New York: Dutton Paperbacks, 1967) is a collection of articles on underground films by critics and filmmakers.

A poster in Japan announces a series of American underground films. (*Jack Newman*)

Most controversy centered around Jack Smith's *Flaming Creatures*. At the Brussels Competition, in December of 1963, Smith's film was shown only, after an apologetic but firm "No" by the screening committee of the Competition, in a crowded hotel room, through which streamed large numbers of the curious, including directors such as Jean-Luc Godard, Agnes Varda, and Roman Polanski.

A similar selection was taken to South America in 1965. And there have been two major exhibitions in Japan, and one in Germany.

In Canada, the films have been seen primarily through the efforts of Guy L. Coté. He collects prints in America and rents them to Canadian film societies.

The initial reactions have varied from location to location, of course. But the demand from overseas for group shows has now become so heavy that *Film Culture* has had to prepare a set of special screening prints just for international exhibition.

The Audience

As with painters and poets, underground film-makers have always been each other's best audience. Film-makers are the most receptive, naturally, because they are the most tuned-in visually. But a wider audience is being sought, for the films *are* made to be seen.

This audience, it is now being proved, does exist. It is made up primarily of people interested in the arts. And students. It is not always a sympathetic audience. But it is one that pays to see the films, that learns from them, and that comes to have a wider viewpoint as to what film may be.

This growing audience, with its attention and its support, has begun to make the term "underground," when applied to a work of personal film art, outdated and meaningless.

SIX: Expanded Cinema

A whole new area of film and film-like art has appeared in the sixties: *expanded cinema.*

Expanded cinema is not the name of a particular style of film-making. It is a name for a spirit of inquiry that is leading in many different directions. It is cinema expanded to include many different projectors in the showing of one work. It is cinema expanded to include computer-generated images and the electronic manipulation of images on television. It is cinema expanded to the point at which the effect of film may be produced without the use of film at all.

Its work is more spectacular, more technological, and more diverse in form than that of the avant-garde/experimental/underground film so far. But it is less personal.

Avant-garde/experimental/underground films are produced primarily in the way that all films have been produced (in the way that even the films of Lumière and Méliès were produced). They are (1) conceived, (2) directed and photographed, (3) edited into more or less permanent form, and (4) projected for an audience from one projector onto one screen. And as rich in potential as this time-honored process is, it is still limited. Therefore the artists have attacked it, have fragmented it, and have destroyed the old idea—that the motion picture is a static work, that it is exactly the same work every time it is shown, and that motion pictures should be made to universal specifications so that they may be shown on given machines under given and never changing conditions. If these ideas ever were true, they are on the way out now. And liberated from the concept of standardization, the personal art film in America has pushed on into a fourth avant-garde.

Expanded cinema may be considered a fourth avant-garde in that many of the underground film-makers are working in this area. But avant-garde/experimental/underground film is only one of the sources of expanded cinema. What has changed cinema to expanded cinema has been nothing less than the development of whole new conditions and sensibilities spreading across all the arts.

The Mutating Factors

To begin with, art has become more aggressive in general. The painter is no longer satisfied with just a small canvas. He wants a large canvas, a wall, then four walls. The same with sculptors and other artists. Artists now want their works to be environments, to be big as life, and in many cases, literally to be life. This implies control of many factors that artists had previously concerned themselves with only on a limited basis—the space around a work, the light operating in that space, and so on.

Likewise, artists have come to want to work in more than one medium, not just in painting, not just in sculpture. Artists want to work in many media, and to combine many media in one work. When the latter is done, an artist is said to be working in mixed media or *inter-media*. Expanded cinema works are often inter-media works, for they sometimes include the use of live performers, television, dance, painting, and various other media combined in what is sometimes called a *media-mix* or *cinema-combine*.

Another factor is that modern technology has been providing new materials for art, materials such as television and videotape, computers for use in animation, stroboscopes, and so on. Most of the new devices used in expanded cinema have been around for ten and more years. But now the artist has more money and more status, and therefore more access to these materials. Also, as man's existence becomes more involved with technology, the artist thinks more naturally of including it in his work. In the 1966 Armory Show, called 9 *Evenings: Theatre and Engineering*, artists collaborated with engineers from AT&T's Bell Laboratories to produce art works utilizing such things as infrared television and Doppler sonar.

Still another element in the development of expanded cinema, especially in color instruments and light shows, is the recent advent of so-called consciousness expanding drugs. It is desirable to have a maximum of visual (and other) sensations while under the influence of LSD. Many cinema environments and light shows are originated to simulate the effect of a psychedelic "trip." This has led to research into older and even ancient methods of the manipulation of light.

Multiple Projection

The most obvious variation on the conventional cinema process is to add more than one set of images by adding more projectors. (Commercial cinema, of course, frequently uses multiple images by putting them all in a single frame of film.) The first to use more than one motion-picture projector for one work may have been Abel Gance in his film "triptych" *Napoléon,* produced in 1925. This film featured three different projectors projecting onto three different screens. Gance later produced other three-screen works, calling the process "Polyvision."

One of the earliest of American multiple-projection works was *Sample Lesson* (1951, 1953). Charles and Ray Eames, Alexander Girard, and George Nelson were commissioned to do an art curriculum study for the University of Georgia. When they presented their *Sample Lesson* at the University of Georgia, and two years later at U.C.L.A., it was partially in the form of film projections that appeared all over the lecture hall. Odors, too, were used in this presentation. A picture of toast, for example, brought the smell of toast, produced by toast being scraped into the air-conditioning system. This was not an attempt to make an experimental film; it was simply the most effective way of communicating the most essential (and sensual) information in the least time. The Eameses later went on to make other multiple-projection works: *Glimpses of the U.S.A.* (1959), *The House of Science* (1962), and *Think* (1964); the first for presentation in Moscow, the second for the Science Pavilion at the Seattle World's Fair (where it is still running every two

Charles Eames and staff did *Glimpses of U.S.A.* with multiple projection to give the Russians an idea of the size and variety of America.

This scene in *The House of Science*, by Eames, shows six different shots of Lick Observatory simultaneously, a sort of instant montage.

Eames used many different images at once to communicate the idea of "two" in the IBM presentation called *Think*.

hours), and the third for the IBM Pavilion at the New York World's Fair. Each was designed for a special architectural environment, the most spectacular of which was the IBM Pavilion. In this structure the theatre was sixty feet above the ground. The audience got into a "people wall" and was hydraulically hoisted the full sixty feet into the film presentation, which included seventeen screens, a live announcer, and a real, roaring motorcycle.

When Kenneth Anger shot *Inauguration of the Pleasure Dome* in 1954, he photographed extra footage for a three-screen version, not shown until 1958. This was perhaps the first excursion of the underground into multiple projection. It was probably not until 1965 that there was extensive exploration of multiple projection for use in personal art expression. And it was in November of 1965 that the Film-makers' Cinematheque presented New Cinema Festival One, bringing together many expanded-cinema works for the first time.

Among those exhibiting was Stan VanDerBeek. VanDer-Beek had, at the time, already begun construction of his Movie-Drome, the hemispheric movie theatre at his home in Stony Point, New York, that is designed specifically for multiple-projection films. In the Movie-Drome thirty people can lie with their heads toward a central projection control, somewhat like a planetarium projector complex, and their feet toward the continuously curving wall/screen. The screen surface is then filled with images from both slide, motion-picture, and overhead projectors. Many of the productions VanDerBeek has exhibited at the New Cinema Festival were rehearsals for Movie-Drome works, which he calls "movie-murals" and "newsreels of dreams." In *Feedback # 1*, he used three screens, placed different distances and angles from the six projectors, which showed slides, documentary footage, and his collage films. Another piece, called *Move-Movies*, utilized not only multiple projection from behind the audience, but five tiny portable projectors carried around the audience. VanDerBeek believes that by using multiple projection one could build a universal visual language for communication among cultures.

Another producer of multiple-projection works is a group called USCO (an abbreviation for Us Company). Their *Hubbub* is a "multi-channel media-mix of films, tape, oscillo-

Stan VanDerBeek and assistants huddle with portable movie projectors in *Move-Movies* as a parade marches upside down in the background. (*Peter Moore*)

scope, stroboscope, kinetic and live images." In terms of equipment, it uses four channels of sound, six slide projectors, two 8mm and two 16mm film projectors, many of which are operated in automatic synchronization from a programmed control center. *Hubbub* has many different sections, and includes, when possible, live performers. There is much random combining of Eastern mystical symbols and sights, natural scenes photographed through diffraction lenses, and words and signs thrown together into a vague kind of poetic relationship. Whimpers of human ecstasy are mixed with roars from motorcycles, and there are views of journeys on a human body landscape and of motorcycle trips. The presentation is very loud and works to increase perception, USCO says, by "sensory exercise and overloading of the senses." Its effects have been called pyschedelic, although the terminology it uses to describe itself and its work is technological in origin. USCO is a group of artists and technicians leading a communal life in Garnersville, New York. Supposedly anonymous, they are led by Gerd Stern, a former public relations man from San Francisco, who was "turned on" to the possibilities of media by reading a Marshall McLuhan report while laid up in a hospital. The first USCO presentation was in 1963, at the San Francisco Museum of Art, and they have been touring ever since, their elaborate equipment purposely portable.

Andy Warhol did not move into multiple projection until 1966. His first excursion was something called *Up Tight*, which later developed into *The Exploding Plastic Inevitable*. These presentations were two side-by-side films, and were combined with stage performances by singers, dancers, and a rock and roll group called The Velvet Underground. Warhol later used the two-simultaneous-movies format in *The Chelsea Girls*, his underground hit, which was probably the first expanded cinema film to be shown in a commercial movie theatre in the United States.

Many other film-makers have been working with multiple projection, among them George Manupelli, Don Snyder, and Barbara Rubin. Snyder especially uses an interesting variation. For screens, he uses piles of cardboard boxes painted white. These boxes are moved around by dancers during the piece, and then hurled into the audience. Projections are turned on the audience, which, half-buried under the boxes, may manipulate these individual "screens" in the light of the projected images.

Film/Dance and Film/Theatre

As does USCO, as does Snyder, many producers of expanded cinema use live performers in their presentations. This idea is not entirely new; for example, the 1909 animated cartoon *Gertie the Dinosaur* was meant to be used in vaudeville theatres in coordination with a live "straight man" who would ask Gertie questions and toss her a pumpkin, and so on.

Inter-media works of a film/dance and film/theatre nature usually involve the interlocking of filmed versions of on-stage actions with those actions. VanDerBeek's *Pastorale: Et Al*, with dancing by Elaine Summers and Bert Supree, has dancers carrying screens and dancing in combination with details of them dancing on film. Ed Emshwiller has a dance piece called *Body Works* in which the dancers, dressed in white, serve as screens. And on them are projected images of themselves. Emshwiller performs this piece by hand-holding the projector. Out of the on-stage movements, the on-film movements, and movement given by Emshwiller's movement of the projector comes a film/dance fugue.

Dancers show up in some form in many productions, including those of Piero Heliczer, Jackie Cassen, Al Hansen, Angus MacLise, Don Snyder, USCO, and Roberts Blossom.

Performers in Ken Dewey's Action Theatre presentation of *Sames* do not move at all. They are five girls standing still in bridal gowns while the lighting intensity changes around them. Across the ceiling of the theatre, however, are projected movies of girls in bridal gowns doing all sorts of activities.

Most Happening artists are in some way involved with film, but the one most oriented toward expanded cinema is probably Robert Whitman. Whitman usually refers to his works as "theatre pieces," not as Happenings. These theatre pieces have live performers working with spaces filled with controlled light and various materials. Film is one of the materials that bounds the spaces. Sometimes it is film shot by Whitman; sometimes it is a print of a travelogue or medical film that he has purchased. Whitman says film can flatten

It is difficult to tell who is real and who is projected in this photograph of Ed Emshwiller's *Body Works* dance/film piece. (*Peter Moore*)

The action in the "Action Theater Presentation" of *Sames* by Ken Dewey occurs entirely on film on the ceiling, as onstage actresses remain motionless throughout. (*Peter Moore*)

A model is distorted with giant mirrors in Robert Whitman's *Two Holes of Water Three. (Peter Moore)*

things out, make them larger or smaller, change their speed, change their color. He adds that film gives distance, that it "is a rock solid steady unchangeable record of someone looking at something past." His films usually echo or present variations of what is appearing "in person" in a piece. In *Two Holes of Water Two* (1966), for example, there is a movie about frozen water in the form of glaciers, and as the movie is shown, a plastic glacier is blown up on stage. There is also a film of people eating under water, and a live television projection of a girl pouring water.

Whitman's earliest theatre piece, *Cannon* (1960), used slides, and he began using film with *The American Moon* (1960), and has used it ever since. In his *Night Time Sky* (1965), given at *The New York Theatre Rally*, his films were projected on a huge tentlike ceiling, rather dominating the piece. He uses a variety of other effects, among them fluorescent light. In one piece a movie screen is actually a fluorescent screen that, when the film is over, traps or "freezes" the shadows of the two performers who stood in front of it while the film was being projected.

Whitman constructed in 1964 a series of "movie pieces." These are objects or environments in which part of the reality is actually on film. *Shower*, for example, has a real metal shower, a real plastic shower curtain, and real water coming down. The person taking the shower, life-size and real looking, is on film. (*Shower* is so real, in fact, that some people seeing it in an art gallery thought they had gone into the wrong room by mistake. They were embarrassed to have barged in on somebody taking a shower.) *Shopping Bag* is a standard paper grocery sack. But inside it is a screen, and on the screen is playing a film of food in various states. Other movie pieces are *Dressing Table, Dining Room Table, Sink*, and *Window*.

Television

"As collage replaced oil paint, the cathode tube will replace the canvas." The cathode tube, of course, is the television tube, and this statement is by Nam June Paik, an artist who is making television art.

Television is like film, but it is not film. When a viewer sees a film he is seeing an image made up of light moderated by shadow, and the texture is of thousands and thousands of tiny grains, usually imperceptible. When he watches television he is seeing an image made up of fluorescent light, and the texture is of hundreds of visible horizontal lines. The quality of image is different. The quality of the television image is of immediacy, and never of spectacle (film); of flow, and never of stability (film). Films are frequently run on television, but then their effect is not of film, but of television.

Robert Whitman uses television in his theatre pieces to show actions that are being performed in the same area as the audience but not in plain sight. Whitman says, "A (television) camera on anything brings it in live—a local news-flash." He has the images of events piped in and then projected on a wall via a special television projector. When blown up to ten feet tall, the normal television image becomes one of a foggy dream. Paradoxically this dream looks more "actual," more like it is really something happening than anything on film.

The television projector is used by other artists, too. In Alex Hay's 1966 Armory Show piece, *Grass Field*, a camera televised his face, and behind him the television image of it was projected to enormous size, all while special microphones were picking up the sounds that his internal organs were making. Robert Rauschenberg used the projector in his Armory work called *Open Score*. Much of *Open Score* was performed in darkness, but, according to Rauschenberg's notes, was "observed and projected by infrared television on large screens for the audience. . . . The conflict of not being able to see an event that is taking place right in front of one except through the reproduction is the sort of double exposure of action. A screen of light and a screen of darkness."

Television images may be manipulated optically with lenses during the "taking" of the image. After that it must be done electronically, and it is probably in electronic manipulation that television's unexplored potential as an art form lies.

Nam June Paik, a Korean now living in New York City, is working with direct electronic manipulation. Actually Paik is involved in the wider field of "electronic art," and has invented such things as a color piano and human-sized

A live television image of Alex Hay's face is projected behind him as Robert Rauschenberg enters from right in *Grass Field*. (*Peter Moore*)

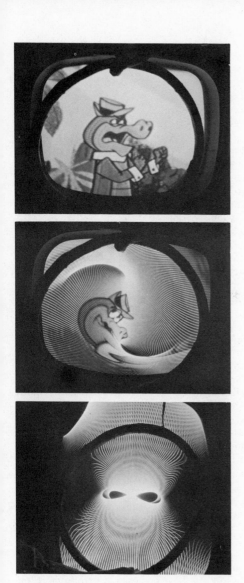

An electro-magnetic field interferes with a television set's "normal" operation and turns a cartoon into an op art pattern in this demonstration by Nam June Paik. (*Peter Moore*)

robots. Paik works with television in several ways. He may adjust the interior mechanism of a set so that it shows a garbled, but aesthetically pleasing image. Or he may interfere with the cathode ray beam of the television tube via a powerful electro-magnet, making its electrons trace force-field patterns across the picture tube. And working with a videotape recorder, Paik may record from many different television channels to make a television collage on tape. He also, of course, can perform electro-magnetic manipulations on the videotape recorder.

Videotape is fairly new, the first such recorder having been developed in 1956 by Ampex. Size, complexity, and cost have gone way down since that time. Videotape allows instant replay, and it makes television tangible enough for the artist to work with. Commercial broadcast equipment is especially versatile, with such features as computer-programmed optical effects. Artists, however, usually do not get their hands on such equipment. An exception occurred when CBS allowed Stan VanDerBeek to put together a videotape work with the help of their engineers for broadcast on a program about underground films. The result, *Panels for the Walls of the World # 1* (1965), closely resembled such VanDerBeek film works as *Breathdeath* and was really a film done with videotape.

Man Ray, maker of some of the earliest avant-garde films, said recently that if he were young now, it would be videotape, not film, that would interest him. Previous generations have grown up watching movies, thinking movies, and living fantasy lives imagined as movies. Currently a whole generation is growing up watching television, thinking television, and living fantasy lives imagined as television. As videotape becomes more and more accessible, this generation will probably use it to create personal television art. Or, in other words, underground television.

Computer Films

Computers are now being used to generate film images, both in industry and in art. In every case, a computer is fed a mathematical program that instructs it to "draw" a certain pattern on a cathode ray tube by means of various X and Y coordinate systems. When the picture is on the screen, the

These four frames were produced when Stan VanDerBeek programmed a computer to produce calligraphic variations on the word "human" for his *When in the Course Of*.

computer triggers the camera. Thus one frame of a computer film is made. The program calls for a series of frames, of course, thus producing animation.

One of the first artists to use computers for film work is John Whitney, one of the Whitney brothers who made the well-known *Film Exercises* in the forties. Whitney rebuilt a war surplus analog computer and "mated" it with an optical printer. This set-up allows him to make any letter, word, or figure go through a variety of symmetrical mutations. A collection of such effects can be seen in his *Catalogue* (1961). His brother James used a similar set-up in the making of *Lapis* (1963–66). John Whitney has gone on to work with the more advanced digital type of computer. He is engaged in a comprehensive study of formal and design problems, working from the point of view that the computer is the ultimate instrument for composing abstract design in motion.

Stan VanDerBeek has also been working with a digital computer, and has produced two films with it. The first is a series of abstract configurations that he has grouped together under the title *Collide-oscope* (1966). The second is a study in calligraphic variation, using the words in the first paragraph of "The Declaration of Independence." This is called *When in the Course of* (1966–67).

Whitney is in California, VanDerBeek in New York. Computer films are being made all over the United States and abroad. So far they are all animated films. Because they have been little seen as yet, it is difficult to know much about their present range or future potential.

Variations on the Theme of Film

It is possible to use materials other than film to produce the approximate effect of film. There is television, of course. There are color instruments and overhead projectors. And there is the shadow play.

Shadow plays have been given in Asia for perhaps thousands of years. Light plays were put on at the Bauhaus in Germany between the Wars, combining human forms, shadow effects, and projection.

Film-maker Ken Jacobs has always sought a sense of immediacy in his film work, and this has led him to the medium of the shadow play. The movie image is a shadow

of an image photographed from life, while the shadow play
is a step nearer to life, being a shadow of life itself. Thus
Jacobs has actors perform in front of lights, but behind a
screen. Their shadows, seen by the audience on the other side
of the screen, form the movie. Location and size of the
shadow image is controlled by location of light sources. It is
possible to have "close-ups" and "long shots." And by manipulating the light sources in certain ways, it is possible to have
cuts, and dissolves, and even multiple-imposition. Jacobs's
first such play was called *Thirties Man: Chapter One of the
Big Blackout of '65*. Other chapters have followed.

Since his first shadow plays, Jacobs has worked on other
film variations. One is a special projector that can project
live objects so that they appear to have three dimensions
even on the two-dimensional screen. And when actually
working with film, Jacobs likes to use a projector that can be
run forward or backward at any speed, thus giving film some
of the element of immediate control that a shadow play
gives.

Nam June Paik uses a film projector, but the film he runs
through it is absolutely clear. He then stands in front of the
projector light, meditating or performing some simple act,
declaring in this way that he is, in that moment, a living
movie. This is called *Zen for Film*. And Paik has other ways
of putting real life into movies. At the New Cinema Festival,
while Paik projected VanDerBeek's *Breathdeath* onto a
paper screen, shaping with his hands the projected image,
the screen ripped slightly, and a girl's long red hair fell out
of the screen, seemingly growing out of the film itself.

A colleague of Paik's, Japanese composer Takehisa Kosugi,
has a piece in which he ritually destroys or purifies the film
medium. He runs a film projector that has no film in it, focus-
ing on a paper screen. He then cuts out the very center of
the screen. And strip by strip, cuts out more and more of
the middle of the screen. In the end there is no screen left,
and the flat glare of light on screen has turned into a deep
light/space. Kosugi calls this *Film & Film # 4*. He and Paik
have many such abstract pieces, in which light and time are
treated as almost tangible materials.

Still another variation on film exists in Standish Lawder's
March of the Garter Snakes. This piece is actually a sequence of slides shown through color-changing polaroid

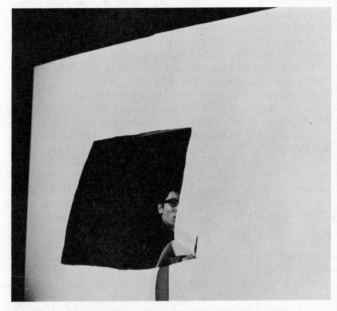

Takehisa Kosugi "destroys" a film, cutting the screen away strip by strip, in *Film & Film #4*. (*Peter Moore*)

lenses. Toward the end, however, the slides actually come alive on the screen. They begin to bubble. Their patterns begin to change, and all their colors to mix. These final slides are actually slide "sandwiches." Two pieces of slide glass are put together with various colored materials sandwiched in between. When the slide sandwich is left in the projector, it gets hot, and the middle part melts, causing the slide picture to turn into a motion picture.

Light Art

The live manipulations of light and color have become increasingly popular in the last few years. Light art did not evolve from cinema, however. Rather cinema and light art have common ancestors, for the practice of light manipulation goes back thousands of years.

Egyptian temples, for example, were constructed so that shafts of light would hit certain points during certain times. And it is believed that priests in ancient Greece and Rome used reflectors to project apparitions of the gods on screens of steam and smoke. At the same time, long before Edison or Lumière, shadow plays that looked like motion pictures were seen in Asia. Later there were primitive projectors that could show slides. These, too, were used to conjure up apparitions, and also to entertain via magic lantern shows.

Color Instruments

"Color organs," developed in the nineteenth century, were instruments that allowed their operators to produce colors the way an organist would musical notes. An early such device, in Paris, had tinted glass "pipes" inside which were burning gas jets. How high or bright the flame in a given pipe burned was controlled from a keyboard, and as each pipe was a different color, one could play compositions with it. Color organs existed in England, Germany, France, and America. Some were portable and were used to give touring color concerts. A. Wallace Rimington, Mary Hallock Greenwalt, A. B. Klein, Rosinee, and Lazlo all worked with such instruments.

The pioneer of color instruments in America was Thomas Wilfred, who began experiments in 1905. By 1921, he had produced his "Clavilux," a keyboard instrument that projected what Wilfred calls a "lumia" composition. Wilfred has made many lumia works. One of the latest, *Lumia Suite Opus 148* (1963–64), may be seen in the special gallery constructed for it at the Museum of Modern Art in New York. It appears on an automatic Clavilux that the still-active Wilfred built for the museum.

Following Wilfred's early work, many color and light instruments have been developed in the United States. One that became well known was Cecil Stoke's 1942 "Auroratone," which made color patterns in response to music vibrations. The source of Auroratone forms was polarized crystal plates. There is a contemporary version of this process, Bob Beck's "The Crystal Trip." Other contemporary American color instruments, by Dr. Henry Hill, Tony Martin, Jim Morrissett, Bob Williams, Jackie Cassen, Earl Reiback, Nam June Paik, and Richard Aldcroft are now in use.

The one that has attracted the most attention is Aldcroft's "Infinity Projector." This is a kaleidoscopic projector that produces a continuous flow of six-sided designs. The designs can be observed on a screen, or one may look directly into the lens of the projector itself. In the latter situation, the viewer wears huge goggles that interfere with the normal coordination of the eyes, causing each eye to see a different image. The difficulty the mind has in reconciling the two images is said to add to the experience.

Light Shows

The early color organs and their successors have now expanded into the light show, which often takes the form of an all-out assault on the senses. Light shows are usually given in conjunction with rock and roll concerts and dances. They draw crowds of a thousand and more.

Light environments and theatres were planned at the Bauhaus, but evidently were never executed. Light environments are now being produced by artists in Europe, but these do not resemble the American variety.

The early light shows, in the fifties, were modest affairs, frequently restricted to overhead projection of liquid tables. In this process, known as the "wet show" process, various dyes and other colored materials are mixed together in water in a shallow glass dish. Their flowing color patterns, which may be controlled in numerous ways, are projected onto a screen or wall. This was originally done to jazz or poetry.

The first spectacular presentations of light art were probably the *Vortex Concerts*, given in San Francisco's Morrison Planetarium from 1957 to 1959. *Vortex* started as environmental concerts of modern music presented by electronic composer Henry Jacobs. Soon, however, Jordan Belson was added as visual director. Belson used up to seventy projectors, slide, film, and strobe, in a fifty-minute performance. *Vortex* had little in common with the present-day light shows. (Belson says that it was the first sign of an art form that has not yet materialized.) It featured precisely programmed sequences of "hard-edged" images, and it was totally controlled.

The contemporary light show is of sprawling dimensions. Its content varies but is usually, at best, loosely combined. There may be overhead projections of liquid tables, slides of "op art" patterns, film loops, stroboscopes, and ultraviolet lamps under which some of the audience paint each other with fluorescent paint. And on the East Coast, television projection is used.

The light show seems to be a West Coast invention. Its origin in time and place, the late fifties in North Beach and West Venice in California, strongly coincides with the beginning of widespread use of hallucinogenic drugs. (The names for light events, *Freak Out, The Acid Test,* and *Trips Festival,* usually have psychedelic connotations. And aficionados of light art call themselves "color heads.") The patterns that one sees in a light show are said to be similar to what the eye sees when a person is under the effect of LSD.

In 1965 and 1966 the light shows expanded in size on the West Coast to where they were being presented in large auditoriums. On the East Coast they were presented in so-called psychedelic discotheques, such as The World and Bob Goldstein's Lightworks. The emphasis on both coasts seems to be on expansion of spectacle, although there have been some moves toward achieving control. Tony Martin, for example, who has been accompanying electronic music with light at the San Francisco Tape Center since 1961, has a lighting control system that completely synchronizes light to sound by circuiting so that his light sources "hear" and respond to sounds.

There is already a bookful of light artists working. (Whereas the underground film-maker went the starving artist route, a good "lights man" averages a hundred dollars per weekend.) Two of the pioneers are said to be Elias Romero and Bill Ham, both from San Francisco. And others in the Bay Area are Ben Van Meter, Roger Hillyard, Tony Martin, Dan Bruhns, Jerry Abrams, Glenn McKay, Bob Holt, and Harold Adler. In Los Angeles there are Dennis Wier, Bob Beck, and Jean Mayo. And in New York there are Bob Goldstein, Harvey Kramer, Rudi Stern, and Jackie Cassen.

Kinetic Art

Not surprisingly, there is a strong tie-up between kinetic artists and expanded cinema. It is the kinetic artists in Europe who have been creating light environments, the newer color instruments, and light effects on sculpture. American film-maker Robert Breer is often classed as a kinetic artist, and so is Len Lye.

Lye, who is credited as being the first to paint the movie directly on the film stock, found the film medium too expensive to make the films he really wanted to make. He therefore switched to kinetic sculpture (a medium he later also found to be too expensive). In Lye's sculptures, strips, rods, or rings of metal are given motion by motors. Impelled to movement, the metal moves in certain patterns, and under light the patterns form shapes. The shapes change as the energy, i.e., motion given by motor, is varied, and as the light is varied. (The whirring and cracking metal creates its own sound track.)

Len Lye working in metal is concerned with much the same materials as Len Lye working in film. He is manipulating light in coordination with time.

Past, Present, Future

The forms of cinema are proliferating. Every new way of creating or controlling light is potentially a new form of cinema.

Metal, film, magnetic tape, cathode tubes, living bodies,

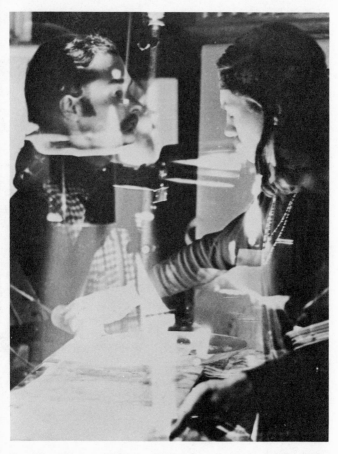
Ben Van Meter and Roger Hillyard perform their light show
in San Francisco's Avalon Ballroom.

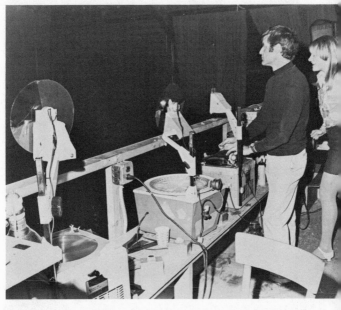

Jim Morrissett sets up overhead projectors for the light show at Cheetah in Los Angeles. (*Bob Beck*)

Morrissett's "lights," projected over a rock 'n' roll band, use more patterns than liquid projections. (*Bob Beck*)

Rings of metal placed in motion and reflecting light in Len
Lye's kinetic sculpture *Roundhead* recall the light patterns
and methods of Man Ray's *Emak Bakia*.

plastic, glass, computer: these are materials of cinema, the secondary materials. They provide means to work with the basic materials of cinema—light and time.

It is only light and time that link all the forms of cinema, past, present, and future.

Appendix
Where To Rent the Films

Key to Appendix

m	—minutes
s	—seconds
B&W	—black-and-white
C	—color
Si	—silent
So	—sound
S/T	—sound on tape
W	—for sale only
Z	—believed to be lost

The films mentioned in the text are available for rental, and sometimes sale, from the sources listed below. After the listing of each film, with pertinent information, will be found the symbol for the distribution source or sources for the film. If the film is not in distribution, it may often be rented from the film-maker himself, who usually may be contacted by writing in care of the source of any of his other films.

Prices for the films vary from source to source, and a film available from two separate sources may well have two varying prices. Most of the films average around a dollar a minute, or a little more. A twelve-minute film, for example, usually runs around twelve or fifteen dollars per showing. The older films tend to be less expensive. No matter how short the film, however, it rarely rents for less than five dollars, for it costs the distributor up to four dollars to ship, receive, and inspect a film for each showing.

Each distributor issues a catalogue. These catalogues, which are usually free of charge, will be sent on request. They are handy to have because in addition to the film prices they usually include brief descriptions of the films.

The reader is asked to note that in the listing below it was not possible in some cases to obtain complete classification details. We thought, however, that such information as we had should be listed. We have not included a good many films for which no classification details could be obtained.

A—Audio Film Center (three locations)	10 Fiske Place, Mount Vernon, N.Y. 10550 Telephone (914) 664–5051
	2138 East 75th Street, Chicago, Ill. 60649 Telephone (312) 684–2531
	406 Clement Street, San Francisco, Cal. 94118 Telephone (415) 751–8080
B—Brandon Films (three locations)	221 West 57th Street, N.Y., N.Y. 10019 Telephone (212) 246–4868
	20 East Huron Street, Chicago, Ill. 60611 Telephone (312) 337–2855
	244 Kearny Street, San Francisco, Cal. 94108 Telephone (415) 397–4255 or 397–0568
CC—Canyon Cinema Cooperative	58 Verona Place, San Francisco, Cal. 94107 Telephone (415) 781–4719
CF—Contemporary Films (three locations)	267 West 25th Street, N.Y., N.Y. 10001 Telephone (212) 675–7220
	828 Custer Avenue, Evanston, Ill. 60202 Telephone (312) 869–5010
	1211 Polk Street, San Francisco, Cal. 94109 Telephone (415) 775–6285
CS—Creative Film Society	14558 Valerio Street, Van Nuys, Cal. 91405 Telephone (213) 786–8277
D—Film-makers' Distribution Center	175 Lexington Avenue, N.Y., N.Y. 10016 Telephone (212) 889–3848
F—Film-makers' Cooperative	175 Lexington Avenue, N.Y., N.Y. 10016 Telephone (212) 889–3820
G—Cinema 16 Film Library	80 University Place, N.Y., N.Y. 10003 Telephone (212) 989–6400
J—Janus Film Library	24 West 58th Street, N.Y., N.Y. 10019 Telephone (212) 753–7100
M—Museum of Modern Art Department of Film	21 West 53rd Street, N.Y., N.Y. 10019 Telephone (212) 245–8900
R—Radim Films	220 West 42nd Street, N.Y., N.Y. 10036 Telephone (212) 279–6653

Note: In the listing below the "mm" designated is only that in which the film is available, but it is not necessarily the mm in which the film was originally produced. Also, length, mm, etc., may have been altered since this compilation.

TITLE	MAKER	LENGTH	C or B&W	Si or So	MM	DISTR.
Abstract in Concrete	Arvino	10½m	C	So	16mm	R
Academy Leader	Malanga	45m	B&W	So	16mm	D, F
Achoo Mr. Kerroochev	VanDerBeek	2s	B&W		16mm	D, F
Adjacent Yes, But Simultaneous	Landow		C	Si	8mm	
The Adventures of Jimmy	Broughton	12m	B&W	So	16mm	G, R
L'Age d'Or	Buñuel	65m	B&W	So	35mm	
Ai-Ye (Mankind)	Hugo	24m	C	So	16mm	R
Ala Mode	VanDerBeek	5m	B&W	So	35/16mm	G
All My Life	Baillie	3m	C	So	16mm	A, CC, D, F
Allegretto	Fischinger	3m	C	So	16mm	M
Allegro	McLaren	2m	C	So	35mm	
Allures	Belson	8m	C	So	16mm	J
An American March	Fischinger	3m	C	So	16mm	M
Anaemic Cinema	Duchamp	7m	B&W	Si	35/16mm	M
Analogies No. 1	Davis	9m	C	So	16mm	R
Andy Warhol	Menken	10m	C	Si	16mm	D, F
Anger Aquarium Arcanum	Anger		C	So	16mm	
Anita Needs Me	Kuchar, G.	20m	C	Si	8mm	D, F
Anticipation of the Night	Brakhage	42m	C	Si	16mm	D, F, G
Apassionata Fantasy	Rogers	10m	C	So	16mm	R
Apple	Warhol		B&W	Si	16mm	D, F
Appointment with Darkness	Vickrey	12m	B&W	So	16mm	G
Arabesque for Kenneth Anger	Menken	4m	C	Si	16mm	D, F

TITLE	MAKER	LENGTH	C or B&W	Si or So	MM	DISTRI.
Archangel	Gruen	3m	C	So	16mm	D, F
Are Era	Landow	17m	C	Si	8mm	D, F
Arrière Saison	Kirsanov	270m	B&W	So	16mm	A
The Art of Vision	Brakhage		C	Si	16mm	D, F
Artie and Marty Rosenblatt's Baby Pictures	Jacobs, K.	3½ m	B&W	S/T	8mm	D, F
Assassination	Warhol		B&W		16mm	D, F
The Assignation	Harrington	8m		So	16mm	B
Astral Man	VanDerBeek		B&W			D, F
At Land	Deren	15m	B&W	Si	16mm	G
The Automotive Story	Burckhardt	15m	B&W	So	16mm	D, F
Autumn Fire	Weinberg	23m	B&W	Si	35/16mm	A, CF, M
Autumn Spectrum	Hirsch	7m	C	So	16mm	CS
Avocada	Vehr	30m	C	S/T	16mm	D, F
Award Presentation to Andy Warhol	Mekas, J.	6m	B&W	Si	16mm	D, F
Awful Backlash	Nelson	15m	B&W	So	16mm	CC, D, F
Babo 73	Downey	60m	C/B&W	So	16mm	D, F
Bagatelle for Willard Maas	Menken	5m	C	Si	16mm	D, F
Le Ballet Mécanique (Mechanic Ballet)	Léger	14m	B&W	Si	35/16mm	M
Batman	Warhol					D, F

Title	Maker	Length	Color	Sound	Format	
Baudelarian Capers	Jacobs, K.	30m	C/B&W	So	16mm	D, F
Beat	MacLaine	6m	C	So	16mm	A
Beauty Environment of the Year 2065	Vehr				16mm	D, F
Beauty Number Two	Warhol	70m	B&W	So	16mm	D, F
Becoming	Davis	9m	C	Si	16mm	R
The Bed	Warhol				16mm	D, F
La Belle et la Bête (Beauty and the Beast)	Cocteau	90m	B&W	So	35/16mm	B
Bells of Atlantis	Hugo	10m	C	So	16mm	R
Berlin, the Symphony of a Great City	Ruttmann	70m	B&W	Si	35/16mm	M
The Big O	D'Avino	3m	C	So	16mm	G
Le Bijou	Lee	8m	C	So	16mm	G
Birth of the American Flag	VanDerBeek				16mm	
The Birth of the Robot	Lye	6m	C	So	35mm	
Bitch	Warhol	70m	B&W	So	16mm	D, F
Black and Whites, Days and Nights	VanDerBeek	5m	B&W	So	35/16mm	D, F
Blacktop	Eames	11m	C	So	16mm	M
Blazes	Breer	3m	B&W	So	16mm	D, F, G
Blonde Cobra	Jacobs, K.	25m	C	So	16mm	D, F
Blow Job	Warhol	30m	B&W	Si	16mm	D, F
Blue Moses	Brakhage	11m	B&W	So	16mm	A, D, F, G
Bop Scotch	Belson	3m	C	So	16mm	

TITLE	MAKER	LENGTH	C or B&W	Si or So	MM	DISTRI.
Born of the Wind	Kuchar, M.	20m	C	Si	8mm	D, F
Branding (Breakers)	Ivens	25m	B&W		35mm	
Breakaway	Conner	3m	B&W	So	16mm	CC, D, F
Breathdeath	VanDerBeek	15m	B&W	So	35/16mm	CS, D, F
Breathing	Breer	3m	B&W	So	16mm	D, F, G
The Bridge	Ivens	15m	B&W	Si	35/16mm	M
Bridges-Go-Round	Clarke	3½m	C	So	16mm	CF, D, F
The Brig	Mekas, J.	68m	B&W	So	35/16mm	D, F
Brothel	Vehr		C			D, F
Brumes d'Automne	Kirsanov	10m	B&W	Si	16mm	A
Bullfight	Clarke	9m	C	So	16mm	D, F
Buzzards over Baghdad	Smith, J.				16mm	
The Cabinet of Doctor Caligari	Wiene	55m	B&W	Si	35/16mm	A, B, CF, CS, M
The Cage	Peterson	25m	B&W	Si	16mm	G
Cambridge Diary	Malanga					D, F
Camera Makes Woopee	McLaren	15m	B&W	Si		
Camp	Warhol	70m	B&W	So	16mm	D, F
Caravan	Belson	3½m	C	So	16mm	
Carnival	Vickrey	6m	C	So	16mm	B
Castro Street	Baillie	10m	C	So	16mm	A, CC, D, F

Title		Length		Sound	Format	Codes
Catalogue	Whitney, John	5m	C	So	16mm	D, F
Cats	Breer	2m	C	Si	16mm	D, F, G
Cat's Cradle	Brakhage	5m	C	Si	16mm	CS
Celery Stalks at Midnight	Whitney, John	4m	C	So	16mm	D, F, G
Charmides	Markopoulos	15m	C	So	16mm	CS
Chasse des Toches	Hirsch	4m	C	So	16mm	D, F
The Chelsea Girls	Warhol	210m	B&W	So	16mm	D, F
Un Chien Andalou (The Andalusian Dog)	Buñuel/Dali	20m	B&W	Si	35/16mm	A, M
The Child's Hand	Jordan				16mm	
A Christmas Carol	Markopoulos	40m	B&W	Si	8mm	D, F
Christmas on Earth	Rubin	26m	B&W	Si	16mm	D, F
Chumlum	Rice		C	So	16mm	D, F
La Chute de la Maison Usher (The Fall of the House of Usher)	Epstein	55m	B&W	Si	35/16mm	M
Circle	Fischinger	2m	C	So	16mm	M
The Circus Notebook	Mekas, J.				16mm	
Citizen Kane	Welles	119m	B&W	So	35/16mm	B, CF, J
City Symphony	Weinberg				35mm	
Clinic of Stumble	Peterson	16m	C	So	16mm	G
Color and Light No. 1	Davis	10m	C	So	16mm	R
Color Cry	Lye	3½m	C	So	16mm	
Color Dances No. 1	Davis	8m	C	So	16mm	R
Color Designs #1	Latelin	7m	C	Si	16mm	G

TITLE	MAKER	LENGTH	C or B&W	Si or So	MM	DISTRI.
Colour Box	Lye	5m	C	So	35/16mm	M
Colour Cocktail	McLaren	5m	C	Si	16mm	
Come Back Africa	Rogosin	84m	B&W	So	35/16mm	CF
Come Closer	Hirsch	7m	C	So	16mm	CS
Composition in Blue	Fischinger	4m	C	So	16mm	M
Confessions of a Black Mother Succuba	Nelson	16m	B&W	So	16mm	A, CC, D, F
The Connection	Clarke	103m	B&W	So	35/16mm	A, D, F
The Cool World	Clarke		B&W	So	35mm	
La Coquille et le Clergyman (The Seashell and the Clergyman)	Dulac	38m	B&W	Si	35/16mm	M
Corruption of the Damned	Kuchar, G.	55m	B&W	So	16mm	CC, D, F
Cosmic Ray	Conner	4m	B&W	So	16mm	A, CS, D, F, G
Cosmic Ray #1	Conner	3m	C	Si	8mm	CC, W-F
Cosmic Ray #2	Conner	3m	B&W	Si	8mm	CC, W-F
Cosmic Ray #3	Conner	3m	B&W	Si	8mm	CC, W-F
Couch	Warhol	6m	B&W	Si	16mm	D, F
La Course aux Potirons (The Pumpkin Race)	Cohl		B&W		16mm	M
Dance Chromatic	Emshwiller	7m	C	So	16mm	D, F, G

Dance in the Sun	Clarke	9m	C	So	16mm	CF, D, F
Dance Movie	Warhol	45m	B&W	Si	16mm	D, F
Dance of the Looney Spoons	VanDerBeek					D, F
Dawn to Dawn	Berne	40m	B&W	Si	16mm	A
Daybreak and Whiteye	Brakhage	8m	B&W	So	16mm	D, F, G
The Dead	Brakhage	11m	C	Si	16mm	D, F, G
The Dead Ones	Markopoulos		B&W		35mm	D, F
Death and Transfiguration	Davis	10m	C	So	16mm	R
The Death of Hemingway	Markopoulos	12m	C	So	35mm	D, F
The Death of P'Town	Jacobs, K.	7m	C	So	16mm	D, F
Défense d'Afficher	Hirsch	10m	C	So	16mm	CS
Desistfilm	Brakhage	7m	B&W	So	16mm	A, D, F, G
Destiny	Lang	80m	B&W	Si	35/16mm	M
The Devil Is Dead	Linder	20m	C	So	16mm	D, F
Diagonal Symphony	Eggeling	7m	B&W	Si	35/16mm	M
Dime Store	Alexander	7m	C	Si	16mm	G
Dionysus	Boultenhouse	26m	C	So	16mm	D, F
Dirt	Heliczer		C	Si	8mm	D, F
Divertissement Rococo	Hirsch	12m	C	So	16mm	CS
Divinations	de Hirsch		B&W	So	16mm	D, F
Dog Star Man	Brakhage	78m	C	Si	16mm	D, F
(Prelude)		(25m)	C	Si	16mm	D, F, G
(Part One)		(30m)	C	Si	16mm	D, F
(Part Two)		(7m)	C	Si	16mm	D, F

TITLE	MAKER	LENGTH	C or B&W	Si or So	MM	DISTR.
(Part Three)		(11m)	C	Si	16mm	D, F
(Part Four)		(5m)	C	Si	16mm	D, F
Doomshow	Wisniewski	10m	B&W	So	16mm	D, F
Double Jam	Hirsch	4m	C	So	16mm	CS
Dracula	Warhol		B&W		16mm	D, F
Dramatic Demise	Anger	5m	B&W	Si	16mm	
Dream Merchant	Jordan	3m	B&W	So	16mm	
Dreams That Money Can Buy	Richter	85m	C	So	16mm	CF
Drips and Strips	Menken	5m	C	Si	16mm	D, F
The Drum	Brummer	22m	B&W	So	16mm	CS
Drunk	Warhol	70m	B&W	So	16mm	D, F
Du Sang de la Volupté et de la Mort	(see Psyche, Lysis, and Charmides)					D, F, G
Duncan Hines	Goldman		B&W	Si	16mm	D, F
Duo Concertantes	Jordan	9m	B&W	So	16mm	CC, D, F
Dwightania	Menken	7m	C	So	16mm	D, F, G
Eargogh	Lederberg	20m	C	Si	16mm	D, F
Early Abstractions	Smith, H.	14m	C	So	16mm	D, F
Eastside Summer	Burckhardt	45m	C	So	16mm	D, F
Eat	Warhol	13m	B&W	Si	16mm	D, F
Eaux d'Artifice	Anger	80m	C	So	16mm	CS, D, F
Echoes of Silence	Goldman		B&W	So	35/16mm	D, F

Title	Maker	Length	Color	Sound	Format	Codes
8 x 8	Richter	80m	C	So	16mm	CF
Eclipse of the Sun Virgin	Kuchar, G.	6m	C	So	16mm	D, F
Ein Traum de Liebenden	Jordan	11m	B&W	Si	16mm	CC, D, F
Eldora	Markopoulos	10m	C	So	16mm	A, D, F
Ellen in Window Land	Vickrey	17m	B&W	Si	16mm	R
Emak Bakia	Ray		B&W	Si	16mm	A, M
Empire	Warhol	480m	C	So	16mm	D, F
The End	MacLaine	35m	B&W	Si	16mm	A, D, F
The End of Dawn	Warhol	18m	C	Si	16mm	D, F
Energies	Davis	9m	C	So	16mm	R
Eneri	Hirsch	7m	B&W	Si	16mm	CS
Entr'acte	Clair	20m	B&W	So	35/16mm	M
Escape Episode	Anger	27m	B&W	Si	16mm	A, M
L'Étoile de Mer	Ray	15m	C	Si	35/16mm	D, F
Eros, O Basileus	Markopoulos	11m	B&W	Si	16mm	CS
Even as You and I	Barlow, Hay, Robbins, Hirsch		B&W	So	16mm	CF
Every Day Except Christmas	Anderson	40m	B&W	So	16mm	A
Everyman	Baillie	3m	B&W	So	16mm	R
Evolutions	Davis	8m	C	So	16mm	D, F
The Extraordinary Child	Brakhage	10m	B&W	Si	16mm	D, F
Eye Music in Red Major	Menken	4m	C	Si	16mm	D, F
The Eye of Count Flickerstein	Conrad	9m	B&W		16mm	G
Eyewash	Breer	3m	C	Si	16/8mm	D, F, G

TITLE	MAKER	LENGTH	C or B&W	Si or So	MM	DISTRI.
Faces	Warhol				16mm	D, F
Facescapes	VanDerBeek					D, F
The Fall of the House of Usher	Harrington	12m	B&W	Si	8mm	A, CS, M
The Fall of the House of Usher	Watson and Webber		B&W	So	16mm	
Fat Feet	Grooms		C/B&W	So	16mm	D, F
Faucet	Menken		B&W	Si	16mm	D, F
Faulty Pronoun Reference, Comparison and Punctuation of the Participle Phrase	Landow					D, F
La Femme de nulle Part	Delluc					
Feu Mathias Pascale (The Late Matthew Pascal)	L'Herbier	110m	B&W	Si	35/16mm	M
Fièvre	Delluc	40m	B&W	Si	35/16mm	M
15 Song Traits (Song 15)	Brakhage		C	So	8mm	D, F
Film Exercises 4 and 5	Whitneys	12m	C	So	16mm	CS, G
Film Exercise 1 (see Three Abstract Film Exercises)						CS
Film Exercises 2 and 3 (see Three Abstract Film Exercises)						CS
Film in Which There Appear Sprocket Holes, Edge Lettering, Dirt Particles, Etc.	Landow	10m	C	Si	16mm	D, F
Film Magazine of the Arts	Mekas, J.	20m	C/B&W	So	16mm	D, F

Film Study						
(see Forty Years of Experiment in Films)	Richter					
The Filmore Bus	Branaman					
(see Films by Bob Branaman)						
Films by Bob Branaman	Branaman	25m	C	Si	8mm	D, F
Films by Stan Brakhage	Brakhage	5m	C	Si	16mm	D, F
Finland	D'Avino		B&W	Si	16mm	G
Finnegans Wake	Bute		B&W	So	16mm	G
A Finnish Fable	D'Avino	6m	C	So	16/35mm	C
Fire of Waters	Brakhage	10m	B&W	Si	16mm	D, F
Fireworks	Anger	15m	B&W	So	16mm	CS, D, F
First Fear	Brummer	11m	B&W	So	16mm	CS
Fist Fight	Breer	11m	C	So	16mm	D, F, G
Flaming Creatures	Smith, J.	60m	B&W	So	16mm	D, F, G
Fleming Faloon	Landow	10m	C	Si	16mm	D, F
Fleming Faloon Screening	Landow		C	Si	8mm	D, F
Flesh of Morning	Brakhage	25m	B&W	So	16mm	A, D, F
The Flicker	Conrad	45m	B&W	S/T	16mm	D, F, G
Flight	Belson	10m	C	So	16mm	
The Flower Thief	Rice	75m	B&W	So	16mm	A, D, F
Flowers of Asphalt	Markopoulos	10m	B&W	Si	16mm	D, F
A Fool's Haikus	Mekas, J.				16mm	D, F
Form Phases IV	Breer	4m	C	Si	16mm	
Form Phases I	Breer	2m	B&W	Si	16mm	
Form Phases II & III	Breer	7½m	C	Si	16mm	

TITLE	MAKER	LENGTH	C or B&W	Si or So	MM	DISTRI.
Forms in Motion	Pavone	8m	C	So	16mm	CF
Forty Years of Experiment in Film (Contains Diagonal Symphony, Rhythmus 21 and 23, Opus 4, Anaemic Cinema, Film Study, Inflation, Two-Penny Magic, Ghosts Before Breakfast, Dadascope, excerpts from Everything Turns, Dreams That Money Can Buy, 8x8)	Eggeling, Richter, Ruttmann, Duchamp	62m	C/B&W	Si/So	16mm	
Four in the Afternoon	Broughton	15m	B&W	So	16mm	G, R
Fragment of Seeking (Symbol of Decadence)	Harrington	15m	B&W	So	16mm	B, CS
Free Radicals	Lye	5m	B&W	So	16mm	
Freight Stop	Downs	10m	B&W	So	16mm	G
Friend Fleeing	Baillie	3m	B&W	So	16mm	
Galaxie	Markopoulos	90m	C	So	16mm	D, F
The General Line	Eisenstein	76m	B&W	Si	16mm	B
Geography of the Body	Maas	7m	B&W	So	16mm	A, D, F, G
Georg	Kaye	55m	B&W	So	16mm	D, F
George Dumpson's Place	Emshwiller	8m	C	So	16mm	D, F

273

TITLE	MAKER	LENGTH	C or B&W	Si or So	MM	DISTRI.
Happenings I	Saroff	25m	B&W	S/T	16mm	D, F
Happenings II	Saroff	25m	B&W	S/T	16mm	D, F
Hare Krishna	Mekas, J.					D, F
Harlot	Warhol	70m	B&W	So	16mm	D, F
Have You Thought of Talking to the Director?	Baillie	15m	B&W	So	16mm	A, D, F
Henry Geldzahler	Warhol	40m	B&W	Si	16mm	D, F
Himself as Herself	Markopoulos		C		16mm	D, F
The Hobo and the Circus	Chatterton	16m	C	Si	8mm	
Hold Me While I'm Naked	Kuchar, G.	17m	C	So	16mm	CC, D, F
Homage to Jean Tinguely's Hommage to New York	Breer	11m	B&W	So	16mm	G
Horror Dream	Peterson	10m	C	So	16mm	G
Horse	Warhol	70m	B&W	So	16mm	D, F
Horse Over Tea Kettle	Breer	7m	C	So	16mm	D, F, G
Hot House (on same reel with Mozart Rondo 4m total)	Whitney, John		C	So	16mm	CS
Hot Leatherette	Nelson	5m	B&W	So	16mm	CC, D, F
Hotel Apex	Kees	9m	B&W	So	16mm	G
House	Eames	11m	C	So	16mm	CS, M
House of Cards	Vogel	18m	B&W	So	16mm	A
How To Start a Fire	Autant-Lara				45mm	
How Wide Is Sixth Avenue	Burckhardt	7m	C	So	16mm	D, F

Title	Filmmaker	Length	Color	Sound	Gauge	Rental
The Human Face is a Monument	VanDerBeek		B&W	So	16mm	D, F
A Hurrah for Soldiers	Baillie	4m	C	So	16mm	A, D, F
Hurry Hurry	Menken	3m	C	So	16mm	D, F, G
Hymn in Praise of the Sun	Jordan	9m	C	So	16mm	
I Was a Teen Age Rumpot	Kuchars	12m	C	Si	8mm	D, F
The Idyl	Lee	10m	C	So	16mm	C
The Illiac Passion	Markopoulos		C		16mm	D, F
Illusions	Belson	5m	C	So	16mm	
Image by Images IV	Breer	3m	C	So	16mm	D, F
Image by Images I	Breer	240 frame loop	C	Si	16mm	D, F
Image by Images II & III	Breer	7m	B&W	Si	16mm	D, F
Images in the Snow	Maas	29m	B&W	So	16mm	A, D, F, G
Improvisations #1	Belson		B&W	Si	16mm	
In Between	Brakhage	10m	C	So	16mm	A, D, F, G
In the Grip of the Lobster	Smith, J.		C		16mm	
Inauguration of the Pleasure Dome	Anger	39m	C	So	16mm	D, F
Inner and Outer Space	Breer	5m	C	So	16mm	D, F, G
Interim	Brakhage	25m	B&W	So	16mm	D, F, G
Introspection	Arledge	7m	C	Si	16mm	G
Jamestown Baloos	Breer	6m	C/B&W	So	16mm	D, F, G

TITLE	MAKER	LENGTH	C or B&W	Si or So	MM	DISTRI.
Jazz of Lights	Hugo	16m	C	So	16mm	R
Jazz on a Summer's Day	Stern		C	So	35mm	
Jeremelu	Levine	2¾m	B&W		16mm	D, F
Jimmy Witherspoon & Penny Bright	Nelson	3m	C	So	16mm	CC, D, F
Joan of Arc	Heliczer		B&W	Si	16mm	D, F
Les Joyeaux Microbes	Cohl		C	Si	16mm	M
June (Towerhouse)	Cornell and Brakhage	10m				
Kaleidoscope	Eames	4m	C	So	16mm	
Kaleidoscope	Lye	18m	C	So	35mm	
Kino-Pravda	Vertov	50m	B&W	Si	35/16mm	M
Kiss	Warhol	70m	B&W	Si	16mm	D, F
Kitchen	Warhol	5m	B&W	So	16mm	D, F
Kustom Kar Kommandos	Anger		C	So	16mm	CS, D, F
Lapis	Whitney, James	80m	C		16mm	CS
The Last Laugh	Murnau		B&W	Si	16mm	M
The Last Moment	Fejos	18m	B&W	Si	35mm	Z
The Lead Shoes	Peterson		B&W	So	16mm	G
Leisure	Kuchar, G.	26m			16mm	D, F
Lemon Hearts	Zimmerman		B&W		16mm	D, F

Title	Filmmaker	Length	B&W/C	Si/So	Gauge	Codes
The Leopard Skin	Landow		B&W	Si/So	16mm	D, F
The Lester Persky Story– A Soap Opera	Warhol				16mm	D, F
Life and Death of a Sphere (on reel with Dime Store 14m total)	Alexander	14m	C	Si	16mm	G
The Life and Death of 9413—A Hollywood Extra	Florey and Vorkapich		B&W	Si	16mm	A, CS, G, M
Life Lines	Emshwiller	7m	C	So	16mm	D, F, G
The Life of Juanita Castro	Warhol	70m	B&W	So	16mm	D, F
Light Reflections	Davis	15m	C	So	16mm	R
Light Rhythms	Brugière					Z
Lights	Menken					
Lil Picards	Vehr				16mm	D, F
Lips	Warhol		B&W	Si	8mm	D, F
Lisa and Joey in Connecticut: "You've Come Back!" "You're Still Here!"	Jacobs, K.		C	S/T	16mm	D, F
The Little Fugitive	Engel	18m	B&W	So	35mm	D, F
Little Stabs at Happiness	Jacobs, K.	2m	C	So	16mm	CS
Logos	Conger	4m	C	So	16mm	M
The Long Bodies	Crockwell		C		16mm	
Looking for Mushrooms	Conner	3m	C	Si	16/8mm	CC, D, F
Loony Tom	Broughton	11m	B&W	So	16mm	G, R
Lot in Sodom	Watson and Webber	27m	B&W	So	16mm	A, B, CS

TITLE	MAKER	LENGTH	C or B&W	Si or So	MM	DISTRI.
The Lovers of Eternity	Kuchar, G.	25m	C	Si	8mm	D, F
Loving	Brakhage	6m	C	Si	16mm	D, F, G
Lupita	Rodriguez-Soltero					D, F
Lurk	Burckhardt	38m	B&W	So	16mm	CC, D, F
Lust for Ecstasy	Kuchar, G.	45m	C	Si	8mm	D, F
Lysis	Markopoulos	30m	C	So	16mm	D, F, G
Mad Nest	Hirsch	4m	B&W	Si	16mm	CS
Madonna	Kuchar, M.	15m	C	So	16mm	D, F
The Magic Feature	Smith, H.	(see No. 12)				
Mambo	Belson	4m	C	So	16mm	
A Man and His Dog Out for Air	Breer	3m	B&W	So	16mm	D, F, G
Man Is in Pain	Jordan	7m	B&W	So	16mm	A
Man or Mouse	Grooms		C	Si	16mm	D, F
(on reel with Umbrellas Bah 2½m total)						
The Man Who Invented Gold	MacLaine	14m	C/B&W	So	16mm	A
Man with a Camera	Vertov	66m	B&W	Si	16mm	B
Mandala	Belson	3m	C	So	16mm	
Manhatta	Sheeler and Strand	9m	B&W	Si	16mm	M
Mankinda	VanDerBeek	10m	B&W	So	16mm	D, F, G
La Marche des Machines	Deslaw	6m	B&W	Si	35/16mm	M

Title	Filmmaker	Duration	Color	Sound	Gauge	Codes
Mass (for the Dakota Sioux)	Baillie	31m	B&W	So	16mm	A, CC, D, F
Mechanical Principles	Steiner	11m	B&W	Si	35mm	
The Mechanics of Love	Maas and Moore	7m	B&W	So	16mm	A, D, F, G
Meditation on Violence	Deren	12m	B&W	So	16mm	G
Melodic Inversion	Hugo	9m	C	So	16mm	R
Melody of the World	Ruttmann	35m	B&W	So	35mm	
Ménilmontant	Kirsanov		B&W	Si	16mm	A, M
Meshes of the Afternoon	Deren	14m	B&W	So	16mm	G
Messy Lives	Warhol		B&W	Si	16mm	D, F
Meta	Howard					
The Millbrook Report	Mekas, J.		B&W	So	16mm	D, F
Millions in Business as Usual	Burckhardt	13m	C/B&W	So	16mm	G
Minerva Looks Out into the Zodiac	Jordan	6m	B&W	So	16mm	
Ming Green	Markopoulos		C	So	16mm	D, F
A Miracle	Breer and Hulten	18s	C	Si	16mm	D, F
Miracle on the BMT	Burckhardt	22m	B&W	So	16mm	D, F
Mr. Frenhofer and the Minotaur	Peterson	21m	B&W	So	16mm	G
Mr. Hayashi	Baillie	3m	B&W	So	16mm	A, D, F
Moires: Dali/Oster Newsreel	Mekas, J.	3½m	B&W	So	16mm	D, F
A Moment in Love	Clarke	9m	C	So	16mm	CF, D, F
Momma Don't Allow	Richardson and Reisz	22m	B&W	So	16mm	CF
The Monkey	Jordan	3m	C	So	16mm	

TITLE	MAKER	LENGTH	C or B&W	Si or So	MM	DISTRI.
Mood Mondrian	Menken	7m	C	Si	16mm	D, F
Moonplay	Menken	5m		So	16mm	D, F
More Milk, Yvette	Warhol	35m	B&W	So	16mm	D, F
Mort d'un Cerf	Kirsanov	14m	B&W	So	16mm	A
Mosaic	McLaren	5½m	C	So	16mm	CF, CS
Mosholu Holiday	Kuchar, G.					D, F
Mother's Day	Broughton	22m	B&W	So	16mm	R, G
Mothlight	Brakhage	4m		Si	16/8mm	D, F, G
Motion Painting No. 1	Fischinger	11m	C	So	16mm	M
Motion Pictures	Breer	3m	C	So	16mm	G
Mounting Tension	Burckhardt	22m	B&W	Si	16mm	A, CC, D, F, G
A Movie	Conner	12m	B&W	So	16mm	CS
Mozart Rondo (on reel with Hot House 4m total)	Whitney, John		C	So	16mm	M
Musical Poster	Lye	3m	C	So	16mm	D, F
My Hustler	Warhol	70m	B&W	So	16mm	A, M
Les Mystères du Château du Dé	Ray	22m	B&W	Si	16mm	D, F
The Mysterious Spanish Lady	Vehr					
The Naked and the Nude	Kuchars	30m	C	Si	8mm	D, F
Naomi and Rufus Kiss	Warhol		B&W	Si	16mm	D, F
Naomi Is a Vision of Loveliness	Jacobs, K.		C	Si	8mm	D, F

Title	Maker	Length	Color	Sound	Format	Codes
Narcissus	Maas and Moore	48m	B&W	So	16mm	G
Neighbors	McLaren	8m	C	So	16mm	A, CF, CS, G
N.Y., N.Y.	Thompson	15m	C	So	16mm	M
News #3	Baillie	3m	B&W	So	16mm	A, D, F
Newsreel (Port Chicago)	Baillie		B&W	So	16mm	A
Night Crawlers	Goldman		B&W	Si	16mm	D, F
Night Lights & Day Hi's	Branaman		C	Si	16mm	
Night Mail	Watt and Wright	24m	B&W	So	16mm	A, B, CF, M
Nightcats	Brakhage	8m	C	Si	16mm	D, F, G
Night Eating	VanDerBeek			Si	35/8mm	
1941	Lee	5m	C	So	16mm	G
Normal Love	Smith, J.		C	S/T	16mm	D, F
Nosferatu	Murnau	100m	B&W	Si	16mm	M
Not a Case of Lateral Displacement	Landow		C	Si	8mm	D, F
Notebook	Menken	10m	C	Si	16mm	D, F
Notes on the Port of St. Francis	Stauffacher	20m	B&W	So	16mm	R
No. 8	Smith, H.	5m	B&W	Si	16mm	D, F
No. 11	Smith, H.	4m	C	So	16mm	D, F
No. 15	Smith, H.		C	Si	16mm	D, F
No. 5	Smith, H.	6m	C	So	16mm	D, F
No. 4	Smith, H.	6m	B&W	So	16mm	D, F
(in Early Abstractions)						

TITLE	MAKER	LENGTH	C or B&W	Si or So	MM	DISTRI.
No. 14	Smith, H.	25m	C	So	16mm	D, F
No. 9	Smith, H.	10m	C	So	16mm	D, F
No. 1	Smith, H.	5m	C	So	16mm	D, F
(in Early Abstractions)						
No. 7	Smith, H.	15m	C	So	16mm	D, F
No. 6	Smith, H.	20m	C	So	16mm	D, F
No. 10	Smith, H.	10m				
No. 13	Smith, H.	180m	C	So	35mm	D, F
No. 3	Smith, H.	10m	C	So	16mm	D, F
(in Early Abstractions)						
No. 12	Smith, H.	50m	B&W	So	16mm	D, F
No. 2	Smith, H.	10m	C	So	16mm	D, F
(in Early Abstractions)						
Object Lesson	Young	12m	B&W	So	35/16mm	C
Obmaru	Marx	4m	C	So	16mm	CS
October	Eisenstein	(see Ten Days that Shook the World)				
Odds and Ends	Conger	4m	C	So	16mm	CS
Oedipus	Vickrey	12m	B&W	So	16mm	G
The Off-Handed Jape	Nelson	8m	C	So	16mm	CC
Oh Dem Watermelons	Nelson	12m	C	So	16mm	A, CC, D, F

Title		Length	Color	Sound	Format	Code
Oh Life, Woe Story, The A-Test News!	Brakhage	5m	B&W	Si	16mm	D, F
Oiley Pelosa the Pumph Man	Nelson	15m	B&W	So	16mm	CC, D, F
Old and New (see The General Line)	Eisenstein					
On Sundays	Baillie	26m	B&W	So	16mm	A, D, F
On the Bowery	Rogosin	65m	B&W	So	35/16mm	CF
On the Edge	Harrington	6m	B&W	So	16mm	CS
100 Glimpses of Salvador Dali	Mekas, J.				16mm	D, F
The One Romantic Adventure of Edward	Jordan	15m	B&W	So	16mm	A
Onésime Horloger	Durand		B&W	Si	35/16mm	M
Open City	Rossellini	103m	B&W	So	35/16mm	CF
Open the Door and See All the People	Hill	82m	B&W	So	35/16mm	D, F
Optical Poem	Fischinger	(see Forty Years of Experiment in Film)				
Opus films	Ruttmann					
Oramunde	Etting					
Orchard Street	Jacobs, K.		B&W	Si	16mm	
Orphée (Orpheus)	Cocteau	86m	B&W	So	35/16mm	B
Painting and Plastics	Davis	12m	C	So	16mm	R

283

TITLE	MAKER	LENGTH	C or B&W	Si or So	MM	DISTRI.
Panels for the Walls of the World #1	VanDerBeek		B&W	So	16mm & video-tape	CS, D, F
Par Avion	Breer	5m	B&W	Si	16mm	
Parade	Eames	5m	C	So	16mm	M
Paris Qui Dort (The Crazy Ray)	Clair	50m	B&W	Si	35/16mm	M
Particles in Space	Lye	5m	B&W	So	16mm	
Pasht	Brakhage		C	Si	16mm	D, F
Passion in a Seaside Slum	Chatterton	32m	C	Si	8mm	
Pat's Birthday	Breer	15m	B&W	So	16mm	D, F, G
Patterns for a Sunday Afternoon	D'Avino	12m	C	Si	16mm	G
Pause	Warhol		B&W	Si	16mm	D, F
Penny Bright & Jimmy Witherspoon	Nelson	3m	C	So	16mm	CC, D, F
The Pervert	Kuchar, M.	15m	C	Si	8mm	D, F
Pestilent City	Goldman		B&W		16mm	D, F
La Petite Marchande d'Allumettes	Renoir	40m	B&W	Si	16mm	M
The Petrified Dog	Peterson	19m	B&W	So	16mm	G
Peyote Queen	de Hirsch	8m	C	So	16mm	D, F
Phenomena	Belson	6m	C	So	16mm	
Phenomenon #1	VanDerBeek		B&W		16mm	D, F

Title	Director	Sound	Color	Length	Gauge	Notes
Pianissimo	D'Avino	So	C	10m	35/16mm	G
Picnic	Harrington	So	B&W	22m	16mm	B
Pink Swine	Jordan	So	B&W	3m	16mm	A
Plague Summer	Kessler	So	B&W	17m	16mm	A
Plastic Haircut	Nelson	So	B&W	15m	16mm	A, CC, D, F
The Pleasure Garden	Broughton	So	B&W	38m	16mm	R
Poem 8	Etting	Si	B&W	14m	16mm	G
The Poor Little Match Girl	Meyer	So	C		16mm	D, F
Poor Little Rich Girl	Warhol	So	C/B&W		16mm	D, F
Potemkin	Eisenstein	Si	B&W	70m	16mm	B, M
The Potted Psalm	Broughton, Peterson	Si	B&W	25m	16mm	G
Prison	Warhol	Si	B&W		16mm	D, F
Prisoner of Mars	Anger	Si	B&W	11m	16mm	
A Private Moment	Malanga					D, F
Proem	Luce and Tregillus	So	C	10m	16mm	R
À propos de Nice	Vigo		B&W	28m	16mm	CF
Psyche	Markopoulos	So	C	25m	16mm	D, F, G
Puce Moment	Anger	So	C	8m	16mm	D, F
Pull My Daisy	Leslie and Frank	So	B&W	29m	35/16mm	D, F, G
Pussy on a Hot Tin Roof	Kuchars	So	C	12m	8mm	D, F

285

TITLE	MAKER	LENGTH	C or B&W	Si or So	MM	DISTRI.
The Queen of Sheba Meets the Atom Man	Rice			So	16mm	D, F
Quixote	Baillie	45m	C/B&W	So	16mm	A, D, F
Raga	Belson	7m	C	So	16mm	
Rain	Ivens	15m	B&W	Si	16mm	M
Rainbow Dance	Lye	4m	C	So	35/16mm	
Rapt	Kirsanov			So	35mm	
Ray Gun Virus	Sharits		C	So	16mm	D, F
Recherche	Hirsch	8m	C	So	16mm	CS
Recreation I	Breer	2m	C	So	16mm	D, F
Recreation II	Breer	1½m	C	Si	16mm	D, F
Re-Entry	Belson	6m	C	So	16mm	
Reflections No. 11	Davis	7m	C	So	16mm	R
Reflections on Black	Brakhage	12m	B&W	Si	16mm	A, D, F, G
Refractions No. 1	Davis	7m	C	So	16mm	R
Relativity	Emshwiller	38m	B&W	So	16mm	D, F, G
Report	Conner	13m	B&W	So	16mm	A, CC, D, F
Retour à la Raison	Ray	3m	B&W	Si	35/16mm	S, M
Rhythm	Lye	1m	B&W	So	16mm	
Rhythmus 21	Richter	3m	B&W	Si	16mm	
Rhythmus 23	Richter	3m	B&W	Si	16mm	M

(in Forty Years of Experiment in Film)

Title	Maker	Length	Color	Sound	Format	Source
Richard Kraft at the Playboy Club	Landow					D, F
Rien que des Heures	Cavalcanti	45m	B&W	Si	35/16mm	M
Ritual in Transfigured Time	Deren	15m	B&W	Si	16mm	G
Roller Skate	Warhol		B&W	Si	16mm	D, F
The Room	D'Avino	10m	C	So	16mm	G
Salome and Delilah	Warhol	45m	B&W	Si	16mm	D, F
Samadhi	Belson	6m	C	So	16mm	
Le Sang d'un Poète	Cocteau	51m	B&W	So	16mm	A
Saturday Afternoon Blood Sacrifice: TV Plug: Little Cobra Dance	Jacobs, K.	9m	B&W	So	16mm	D, F
Sausalito	Stauffacher	9m	B&W	So	16mm	R
Say Nothing	Noren	30m	B&W	So	16mm	D, F
Scarface and Aphrodite	Zimmerman	15m	B&W	So	16mm	D, F
Scenes from Under Childhood	Brakhage					D, F
Schmeerguntz	Nelson and Wiley	15m	B&W	So	16mm	A, CC, D, F
Science Friction	VanDerBeek	9m	C	So	35/16mm	D, F, G
Scorpio Rising	Anger	31m	C	So	16mm	D, F
Scotch Hop	MacLaine	7m	C	So	16mm	A
Scotch Tape	Smith, J.	3m	C	So	16mm	D, F
Scrambles	Emshwiller	15m	B&W	So	16mm	D, F
Scratch Pad	Hirsch	7m	C	So	16mm	CS

TITLE	MAKER	LENGTH	C or B&W	Si or So	MM	DISTRI.
Screen Test Number One	Warhol	70m	B&W	So	16mm	D, F
Screen Test Number Two	Warhol	70m	B&W	So	16mm	D, F
Screwball	Kuchars	6m	C	Si	8mm	D, F
The Sculpture of David Lynn	Baillie	3m	B&W	So	16mm	
Seance	Belson	4m	C	So	16mm	
The Secret of Wendel Samson	Kuchar, M.	35m	C	So	16mm	CC, D, F
See Saw Seems	VanDerBeek		B&W	Si	16mm	D, F
Senseless	Rice	28m	B&W	So	16mm	D, F
The Sensualist	Goldman		B&W	So	35mm	
Serenity	Markopoulos	70m & 90m	C	So	35mm	
Shadows	Cassavetes		B&W	So	35mm	
Shoot the Moon	Grooms and Burckhardt	28m	B&W	So	16mm	D, F
Shoulder	Warhol	4m	B&W	Si	16mm	D, F
Sidewalks	Menken	5m	C	Si	16mm	D, F
Silent Sound Sense Stars Subotnick & Sender	Brakhage	2m	B&W	Si	16mm	
The Sin of Jesus	Frank	40m	B&W	So	35/16mm	D, F, G
Sins of the Fleshapoids	Kuchar, M.	50m	C	So	16mm	D, F
Sirius Remembered	Brakhage	12m	C	Si	16mm	D, F, G
66	Breer	5m	C	So	16mm	D, F, G
Skin	Linder	12m	C	So	16mm	D, F

Title	Maker	Length	Color	Sound	Gauge	Sources
Skullduggery Part I	VanDerBeek		B&W	So	35/16mm	D, F, G
Skullduggery Part II	VanDerBeek	5m	B&W	So	35/16mm	D, F
The Sky Socialist	Jacobs, K.		C	Si	8mm	D, F
The Slasher	Kuchars	20m	C	Si	8mm	D, F
Sleep	Warhol	360m	B&W	Si	16mm	D, F
Snapshots of the City	VanDerBeek	5m	B&W	So	16mm	D, F
Snow Show	VanDerBeek					D, F
Son of Academy Leader	Malanga					D, F
Song of Ceylon	Wright	40m	B&W	So	35/16mm	B, CF, CS, M
Songs (23 of them)	Brakhage		C	Si	8mm	D, F
La Souriante Madame Beudet (The Smiling Madame Beudet)	Dulac	35m	B&W	Si	35/16mm	M
Space	Warhol		B&W	So	16mm	D, F
Star Spangled to Death	Jacobs, K.		C		16mm	D, F
Still Life	Baillie	2m	C	So	16mm	A, D, F
Stone Sonata	D'Avino	3m	C	So	35/16mm	G
Street Meet	VanDerBeek					D, F
Strike	Eisenstein	90m	B&W	Si	16mm	M, J
A Study in Choreography for Camera	Deren	4m	B&W	Si	16mm	G
Study No. 8	Fischinger	4m	B&W	So	16mm	M
Study No. 11	Fischinger	4m	B&W	So	16mm	M
Study No. 7	Fischinger	2m	B&W	So	16mm	M
Study No. 6	Fischinger	2m	B&W	So	16mm	M

TITLE	MAKER	LENGTH	C or B&W	Si or So	MM	DISTRI.
Subject Lesson	Young	22m	C	So	16mm	G
Suicide	Warhol	70m	C	So	16mm	DF
Summerwind	Dorsky	12m	C	So	16mm	D, F
Summit	VanDerBeek	15m	C	So	35/16mm	D, F
Super Spread	Nelson	11m	C	So	16mm	CC, D, F
Surf and Seaweed	Steiner	11m	B&W	Si	35mm	M
Swain (Rain Black, My Love)	Markopoulos	24m	C	So	16mm	D, F, G
Swinging the Lambeth Walk	Lye	4m	C	So	16mm	M
Synchronization	Jacobs, L. and Bute					
Tarantella	D'Avino	2m	C	So	35/16mm	G
Tarzan and Jane Regained . . . Sort of	Warhol	120m	C/B&W	S/T	16mm	D, F
Taylor Mead Dances	Morrisey	14m	B&W	S/T	35/16mm	D, F
Ten Days That Shook the World	Eisenstein	69m	C	Si	16mm	B, M
Termination	Baillie	5m	B&W	So	16mm	
Texture of Decay	Vickrey	11m	B&W	So	16mm	G
Thanatopsis	Emshwiller	5m	B&W	So	16mm	D, F, G
Thelma Abbey	Anger	10m	B&W	So	16mm	
Theme and Transition	D'Avino	4m	C	So	16mm	
Thick Pucker	Nelson	11m	B&W	So	16mm	A, CC, D, F
The Thief and the Stripper	Kuchars	20m	C	Si	8mm	D, F

Title	Maker	Length	Color	Sound	Format	Rental
Thigh Line Lyre Triangular	Brakhage	5m	C	Si	16mm	D, F, G
Things To Come	Marx	4m	C	So	16mm	CS
The 13 Most Beautiful Boys	Warhol		B&W	Si	16mm	D, F
The 13 Most Beautiful Women	Warhol		B&W	Si	16mm	D, F
This Film Will Be Interrupted After 11 Minutes by a Commercial	Landow		C	Si	16mm	D, F
3	Jordan	8m	B&W	So	16mm	A, CS
Three Abstract Film Exercises	Whitneys	8m	C	So	16mm	CS, G
Three Films (Blue White, Blood's Tone, Vein)	Brakhage	10m	C	Si	16mm	D, F
Thru the Looking Glass	Davis	10m	C	So	16mm	R
Time of the Heathen	Emshwiller/Kass	75m	C/B&W	So	35mm	
Tinsel Tree	Anger	3m	B&W	Si	16mm	
To L.A. . . . With Lust	Zimmerman	27m	C/B&W	So	16mm	D, F
To Parsifal	Baillie	16m	C	So	16mm	A, D, F
Toccata for Toy Trains	Eames		C	So	35/16mm	B
Toccata Manhatta	Rogers		C	So	16mm	D, F, G
Totem	Emshwiller	16m	C	Si	16mm	D, F
A Town Called Tempest	Kuchar, G.	30m	C	So	8mm	M
Trade Tatoo	Lye	6m	C	So	16mm	D, F, G
Transformations	Emshwiller	5m	C	So	16mm	
Transmutation	Belson		B&W	Si	16mm	R
Treadle and Bobbin	Gelentine	8m	C	So	16mm	G
A Trip	D'Avino	2m	C	So	16mm	

TITLE	MAKER	LENGTH	C or B&W	Si or So	MM	DISTRI.
Trumpit	Jordan	8m	B&W	So	16mm	A, CS
Tryptych	Jordan	14m	C	So	16mm	CC
A Tub Named Desire	Kuchars	5m	C	Si	8mm	D, F
Tung	Baillie	9m	B&W	Si	16mm	A, CC, D, F
Tusalava	Lye		C	Si	16mm	
23 Psalm Branch (Song 23)	Brakhage	60m	C	Si	8mm	D, F
Twice a Man	Markopoulos	60m	C	So	16mm	D, F, G
Two: Creely/McClure	Brakhage	5m	B&W	Si	16mm	D, F
Uberfall	Metzner	20m	B&W	Si	35/16mm	
Under the Brooklyn Bridge	Burckhardt	15m	B&W	So	16mm	D, F
Undertow	Jordan	10m	C	So	16mm	A, CS
Unglassed Windows Cast a Terrible Reflection	Brakhage	35m	B&W	Si	16mm	D, F
The Unwelcome Guests	Grooms	8m	C	Si	8mm	D, F
Les Vampires	Feuillade	360m	B&W	Si	35mm	
Variable Studies	Emshwiller	5m	C	So	16mm	
Variations (Early Films)	Whitneys	13m	C	Si	16mm	CS
Variety	Dupont	90m	B&W	Si	16mm	M
Venice Etude No. 1	Hugo	10m	C	So	16mm	R
Vernissage	D'Avino	45m	B&W	Si	16mm	
The Very Eye of Night	Deren	15m	B&W	So	16mm	G

Title	Maker	Length	Color	Sound	Format	Codes
Vinyl	Warhol	70m	B&W	So	16mm	D, F
Visual Variations on Noguchi	Menken	4m	B&W	So	16mm	D, F
Vivian	Conner	3m	B&W	So	16mm	A, CC, D, F
Voyage dans la Lune (A Trip to the Moon)	Méliès	10m	B&W	Si	16mm	A, CS, M
Washington's Wig Wham	Grooms	9m	C	So	16mm	D, F
Water Light	Jordan		C	So	16mm	
The Way to the Shadow Garden	Brakhage	10m	B&W	So	16mm	D, F, G
We Stole Away	Jacobs, K.	3m	C	Si	8mm	
The Weavers	D'Avino		C	So	16mm	
Wedlock House: An Intercourse	Brakhage	11m	B&W	Si	16mm	D, F, G
Weekend	Ruttmann		White	So	35mm	
The Wet Destruction of the Atlantic Empire	Kuchars				8mm	
What Mozart Saw on Mulberry Street	Burckhardt	6m	B&W		16mm	D, F
What Who How	VanDerBeek	8m	B&W	So	16mm	D, F, G
Wheels #4	VanDerBeek		B&W	So	16mm	D, F
Wheeels #1	VanDerBeek	5m	B&W	So	16mm	CS, D, F
Wheeels #2	VanDerBeek	5m	B&W	So	16mm	CS, D, F
Whips	Warhol		B&W		16mm	D, F
Who Has Been Rocking My Dream Boat?	Anger	7m	B&W	Si	16mm	

TITLE	MAKER	LENGTH	C or B&W	Si or So	MM	DISTRI.
Wichita Film	Branaman				8mm	
Window Water Baby Moving	Brakhage	12m	C	Si	16mm	D, F, G
The Winter Footage	Jacobs, K.		C	Si	8mm	
A Woman Distressed	Kuchar, G.	15m	C	Si	8mm	D, F
The Wonder Ring	Brakhage	4m	C	Si	16mm	D, F
The Wormwood Star	Harrington		C		16mm	D, F
Wrestling	Menken	5m	B&W	So	16mm	D, F
Writ in Water	Davis	10m	C	So	16mm	R
Yantra	Whitney, James	7m	C	So	16mm	CS
Yellow Horse	Baillie	8m	C	So	16mm	A, D, F
Yes	Levine	25m	C/B&W	So	16mm	D, F
Yet	VanDerBeek	2m	B&W	So	16mm	
Zen for Film	Paik		White	Si	16mm	D, F
Zenscapes	Menken		C	Si	16mm	D, F
Zig Zag	Stauffacher	7m	C	So	16mm	R
Zone Moment	Brakhage	3m	C	Si	16mm	

Most expanded cinema works can be rented through the Film-makers' Cooperative but are quite expensive as they involve live performers, plus traveling expenses for performers and equipment.

Selected
Bibliography

Barry, Iris. *Film Notes.* New York: Museum of Modern Art, 1939.

Beck, Bob. *Light Show Manual.* Los Angeles: Pericles Press, 1966.

Canyon Cinema News, November, 1966. This publication is available for $2.00 per year at 263 Colgate Avenue, Berkeley, California, 94708.

Film Culture, Numbers 1–43, 1955–1966. This publication is available for $4.00 per year at GPO Box 1499, New York, N.Y., 10001.

Film-makers' Cooperative Catalogue No. 3. New York, 1965.

Jacobs, Lewis. *The Rise of the American Film.* New York: Harcourt, Brace & Co., 1939.

Kirby, Michael. *Happenings.* New York: E. P. Dutton & Co., 1965.

Knight, Arthur. *The Liveliest Art.* New York: The New American Library, Inc., 1959.

Manvell, Roger, ed. *Experiment in the Film.* London: Grey Walls Press, 1949.

McBride, James. *The Contemporary American Avant-garde Program Notes.* New York: The Gallery of Modern Art, 1964.

9 evenings: theatre and engineering. (Program.) New York, 1966.

Pike, Robert Marvin. *A Critical Study of the West Coast Experimental Film Movement.* (Master's thesis.) Los Angeles, 1960.

Sadoul, Georges. *Dictionnaire des Cinéastes*. Paris: Editions du Seuil, 1965.

Stauffacher, Frank, ed. *Art in Cinema*. San Francisco: San Francisco Museum of Art, 1947.

Index

297